Hey Coral,

It was great to meet
and look forward to watching
you help reshape our industry.

Hope you enjoy the read!

Best wishes,

Shift

Shift

Transform Motion into Progress in Business

Richard Lees

Azlan Raj

WILEY

This edition first published 2022

This work was produced in collaboration with Write Business Results Limited. For more information on Write Business Results' business book, blog, and podcast services, please visit our website: www.writebusinessresults.com, email us on info@writebusinessresults.com or call us on 020 3752 7057.

Registered office
John Wiley & Sons Ltd, The Atrium, Southern Gate, Chichester, West Sussex, PO19 8SQ, United Kingdom

For details of our global editorial offices, for customer services and for information about how to apply for permission to reuse the copyright material in this book please see our website at www.wiley.com.

Wiley publishes in a variety of print and electronic formats and by print-on-demand. Some material included with standard print versions of this book may not be included in e-books or in print-on-demand. If this book refers to media such as a CD or DVD that is not included in the version you purchased, you may download this material at http://booksupport.wiley.com. For more information about Wiley products, visit www.wiley.com.

Designations used by companies to distinguish their products are often claimed as trademarks. All brand names and product names used in this book are trade names, service marks, trademarks or registered trademarks of their respective owners. The publisher is not associated with any product or vendor mentioned in this book.

Limit of Liability/Disclaimer of Warranty: While the publisher and author have used their best efforts in preparing this book, they make no representations or warranties with respect to the accuracy or completeness of the contents of this book and specifically disclaim any implied warranties of merchantability or fitness for a particular purpose. It is sold on the understanding that the publisher is not engaged in rendering professional services and neither the publisher nor the author shall be liable for damages arising herefrom. If professional advice or other expert assistance is required, the services of a competent professional should be sought.

Library of Congress Cataloging-in-Publication Data

Names: Lees, Richard (Chief strategy officer), author. | Raj, Azlan (Chief marketing officer), author.
Title: Shift : Transform motion into progress in business / Richard Lees and Azlan Raj.
Description: West Sussex, United Kingdom : Wiley, 2022. | Includes index.
Identifiers: LCCN 2021042852 (print) | LCCN 2021042853 (ebook) | ISBN 9781119810148 (cloth) | ISBN 9781119810506 (adobe pdf) | ISBN 9781119810490 (epub)
Subjects: LCSH: Customer relations. | Consumer behavior. | Consumer satisfaction. | Success in business.
Classification: LCC HF5415.5 .L438 2022 (print) | LCC HF5415.5 (ebook) | DDC 658.8/12—dc23
LC record available at https://lccn.loc.gov/2021042852
LC ebook record available at https://lccn.loc.gov/2021042853

Cover Design: Wiley
Printed and bound by CPI Group (UK) Ltd, Croydon, CR0 4YY

C9781119810148_131221

CONTENTS

6   Turn Headwinds into Tailwinds   173

7   It Will Rain on Your Parade   195

8   Go for the Albatross   235

        Conclusion   265

        Epilogue   271

        About the Authors   279

        Index   285

FOREWORD

At dentsu, we are striving to be champions for meaningful progress. This is one of the core principles that underscores our vision, but what does it truly mean? For us, *meaningful* refers to activities that add value to people's lives, while *progress* is the positive manifestation of motion with the focus placed firmly on our desired outcomes.

Meaningful progress is a force for growth and good. It is a force that can unlock unique possibilities to drive sustainable value and lead to lasting change. It is the gateway to the future for brands in all industries.

I first met Rich and Az after joining dentsu in 2020, and when they shared the concept of this book, I could immediately see how our ambition of championing meaningful progress was woven throughout its chapters. More than this, it maps out the connections that businesses of all sizes must consider if they, too, are to achieve meaningful progress.

In the highly competitive and fast-changing world that we find ourselves in, keeping up is hard enough and staying ahead can be a constant challenge. The currency of business nowadays is speed. Doing "something" is simply not good enough. There are numerous fronts that must be navigated simultaneously, and prioritising the important over the nice-to-have can be hard to do.

This struggle is one that Rich and Az understand well. The ideas they share in this book are simple to draw out. They are easy to explain, and certainly important to connect. However, they are difficult to do, which is why so many businesses get stuck in a trap of constant motion, whereby a lot of tasks are done that keep everyone very busy and deplete budgets, but you lose sight of meaningful progress.

When this happens, it becomes increasingly difficult to translate this movement into clear and measurable business or customer value. This is when the focus often shifts to processes and projects, moving away from customer needs and the value that is derived from meeting them.

Az and Rich use a simple Formula 1 analogy to link the three core themes that a business must connect to create one seamless ecosystem for success. Drawing on their collective 50 years in the realm of customer experience, they use clear examples of the challenges that businesses face in order to highlight not only the importance of each core theme, but more importantly, the need to weave them across every element of the business landscape to deliver true value.

The first of these core themes is a clear vision that sets the direction and common purpose for your organisation, and the need for clear measures to ensure you remain on track. The second is the team and the need for alignment of purpose across an entire organisation. They also delve into radical collaboration, another of our passions at dentsu, as well as the need for autonomy. The final theme relates to reading the market and understanding the external factors that affect every business's ability to compete effectively.

The threads that connect these themes and their many integrated topics are the simple concepts of starting with the end in mind, recognising that motion does not necessarily equate to progress, and actively seeking out and measuring that progress.

If you can't turn motion into progress, what you are left with is a lot of very expensive movement. If you proxy motion for progress, as many businesses do, you will become stuck. As you read, you may realise that your business falls into this category. If that's the case, you'll find tools in these chapters to help you turn motion into meaningful progress. I urge you to use them.

Since starting my role with dentsu, I have spoken to hundreds of clients and all of them mention the same challenges; chief among them are transformation and finding a way to measure the efficiency of their activities. In my career I have been both client and agency side; I have worked with some of the world's biggest brands and I have witnessed how these challenges manifest themselves in different organisational environments. I also understand the crucial role that strong leadership plays in navigating these challenges.

I believe a leader's role is to provide a careful balance between hope and reality. Great leaders paint a vivid picture of what they want to do and where they want to go. They align people and resources around their vision of the future, but they do so without neglecting the reality of where they are now. They are transparent, honest, and realistic about what the journey from their current reality to their visionary future entails. This is the foundation for achieving meaningful progress, and it is these ideas that you will find woven throughout this book in an interesting and thought-provoking way.

The compelling anecdotes and connected themes that are covered in this book are as applicable for marketing leaders as for CEOs.

Dive in, learn what you can from the years of experience Rich and Az bring to this space, and have the courage to invent the future that you're taking your company into. In doing so, you too will become champions for meaningful progress.

Wendy Clark

CEO, dentsu international, and former President, Sparkling Brands & Strategic Marketing, Coca-Cola North America

ACKNOWLEDGMENTS

In our roles, we have been privileged to work with some of the most respected business leaders in the world. These leaders have been kind enough to share their insights with us, and you will see some of their thoughts throughout the book.

Our adaptive leaders

Whilst we had some contributors share their thoughts anonymously, we wanted to thank them and all the individuals below who have shared their thoughts in this book:

Paloma Azulay, Global Chief Brand Officer, Restaurant Brands International

Aaron Bradley, VP of Technology & Innovation, Wella Company

Benjamin Braun, CMO, Samsung

Wendy Clark, Global CEO, dentsu international

Nicholas Cumisky, YouTube

Craig Dempster, Global CEO, Merkle

Doug Jensen, SVP – GTM & COE for Analytics & Activation, Estée Lauder

Nicola Mendelsohn, CBE, VP GBG, Meta

Nick Ratcliffe, Customer Experience Director, Volkswagen Group Ltd

Paul Robson, President of Adobe International, Adobe Craig Smith, Chief Brand Officer & Co-Founder, Decidable Global Ltd, and Former Digital Commerce Director, Ted Baker

Marisa Thalberg, EVP, Chief Brand and Marketing Officer, Lowe's

Deborah Wahl, Global CMO, General Motors

Margaret Wagner, EMEA President, Merkle

Jennifer Warren, VP Global Brand Marketing, Indeed

Shelley Zalis, CEO, The Female Quotient

Our adaptive families

We would like to thank our families for the support they've given us. They've been there through the late nights and the long weekends, being both our samples of one and to ground us when needed. Our wives have kept us going and our children have done their best to keep the noise down whilst we've been working! We definitely wouldn't have made it through this journey without them.

Our adaptive readers

We would also like to thank you, the reader. Our aim was to provide something that was useful to you with a flavour of fun and a sprinkle of our personalities. We hope that the blood, sweat, and tears that we've put into this book (please don't let that sway your opinion) is as enjoyable for you to read as it was for us to write.

INTRODUCTION:
ROCKING HORSES DON'T
BELONG IN BOARDROOMS

"Don't confuse motion for progress. A rocking horse moves all day but goes nowhere"!

– Alfred Montapert

Picture a child sitting on a rocking horse. She is laughing as she sways back and forth. Maybe she is pushing the rocking horse to go faster, encouraging it by shouting phrases like, "Giddy up!" As you watch the child enjoying her ride on the rocking horse, you smile. She is safe; she is happy, and you know that regardless of what her imagination is telling her, she is going nowhere (in the physical sense). You leave her to her game, confident that you won't look out of the window to see her galloping across the garden on her rocking horse in half an hour.

You would certainly think it odd if you walked into a boardroom to see the CEO, CMO, CTO, or any of the other directors sitting on a rocking horse. However, all too often, businesses have boardrooms filled with metaphorical rocking horses; they just don't realise it. They don't always distinguish between *motion* and *progress*, or know how to turn the motion they are generating into progress.

Charting progress in a modern business world

The business world today, especially after black swan events like the 2008 financial crisis or the global COVID-19 pandemic, is characterised by an increasingly big number of known unknowns. It seems clear that the past is probably no longer a safe basis for predicting the future, and much of what we have learned and been taught may well have limited relevance to our future decision making.

The competition feels like it can come from anywhere, and time is definitely no longer on your side. As Rupert Murdoch said (in 1999!), "The world is changing very fast. Big will not beat small anymore. It will be the fast beating the slow".

To not only survive, but to thrive in the new world is a constant challenge that requires businesses to fast become the masters of many things. Agility (speed) and adaptability (ability to change) have become strategic differentiators, giving those businesses that can rapidly adapt and build a muscle to respond to change a massive advantage.

"The speed and availability of data, technology, analytics, content, and platforms is creating this perfect storm where we can finally capitalise on the opportunity presented by the total customer experience in a way that we just couldn't before. If brands are not on that journey to that complete and total customer experience across those dimensions of sales, service, commerce and marketing, they just won't be around in the future."

Craig Dempster, Global CEO, Merkle

Some businesses have the advantage of already being in this state (let's call them the leaders). Others are undergoing massive transformations to close the gap and either attain or regain this state (let call them the followers, who are playing catchup). However, to do this requires sustained and directed momentum, or motion, but motion alone will not give you the advantage. The advantage comes from turning motion into progress.

This might sound simple enough, but often this is more difficult to achieve than it first appears. The result in many businesses is a great deal of motion that adds little real value and instead wastes precious time and resources, and may even contribute to a loss of competitive advantage. The opportunity, as we explain in this book, is to turn that motion into progress. To do that, you need to connect the three core themes of the business ecosystem, which we are calling the principal, the crew, and the season.

The race to the top

Our favourite analogy to describe what a business needs to do in order to turn motion into progress is Formula 1. Behind the fast cars, daring driving, and excitement of race days there are three key components at work: the principal, the crew, and the season.

The principal of each team sets the direction and leads from the front. The crew needs to collaborate and work together to constantly improve the car, its engine performance, drive the car, and find ways to shave even 0.1 of a second off the lap time or length of a pit stop because that 0.1 second can mean the team's driver wins the race. Then there is the Formula 1 season, which lasts for much longer than a single race. Every race throughout the season is different. The car itself will perform differently depending on both the track and the weather conditions on the day, and the crew will need to adapt according to the conditions.

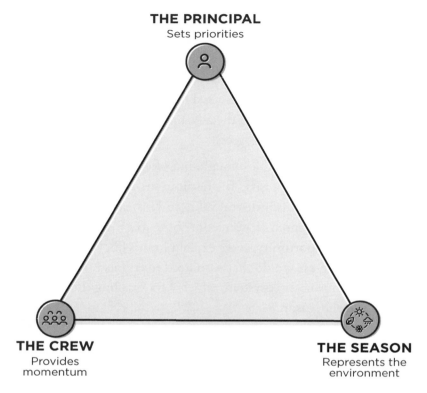

THE PRINCIPAL
Sets priorities

THE CREW
Provides
momentum

THE SEASON
Represents the
environment

Figure i.1

When we apply those three principles to a business, we can see a clear correlation to core enterprise functions and challenges. The principal represents the leaders within the business, the people who make those big decisions, keep one eye on the big picture, and make sure that the company is moving in the right direction. The crew is the broader teams, the people on the ground who make things happen. When they are all aligned behind an organisation's vision, great things happen and progress begins to accelerate.

The season is the external environment that will have an impact on not only how the business performs, but also on how the team functions and performs in different situations. The season is the one element of the pyramid that the business doesn't have total control over. What any organisation can control, however, is how it responds to its environment. This becomes a game of agility, where the businesses that learn fast and adapt quickly survive, and those that don't, die.

You need to have all three components of the pyramid in place and working together in order to achieve progress. Without all of these components, your business will struggle to successfully turn motion into progress.

If you just have the principal with the season, but the crew is not aligned and engaged, you create fatigue. You will only have a short amount of time to build momentum and achieve your goals before you run out of energy.

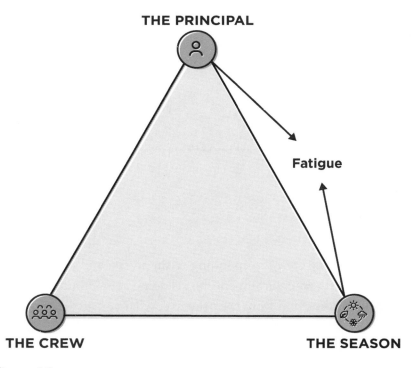

Figure i.2

If you have the principal setting a clear direction of travel and the crew aligned behind them, but no awareness of the season and external environment, this leads to obsolescence. You won't be creating and delivering the products or services the market, and your customers, need.

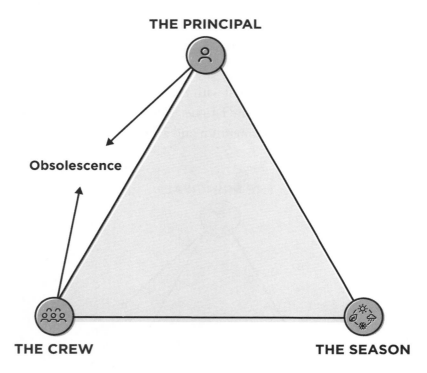

Figure i.3

Finally, if the crew is responding to the season and working within the external environment, but is doing so without any leadership or direction from the principal, what you are left with is chaos. There won't be any coherence in your activities and progress will stall.

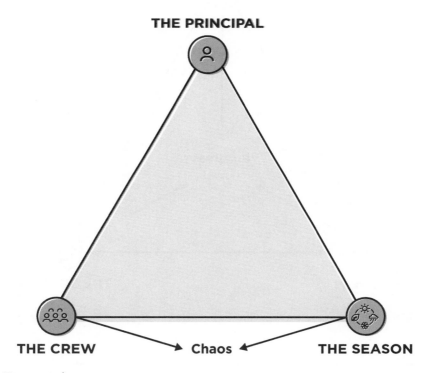

Figure i.4

What many organisations are aiming for is what we discussed at the beginning: the principal setting a clear direction and communicating the big-picture vision; the crew aligning with this vision, buying into it and being given autonomy to work toward that goal; and the organisation as a whole being aware of and having the ability to adapt to an ever-changing environment. The ideal state is to find a balance among all three themes.

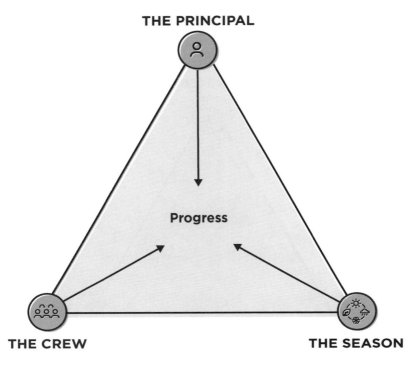

THE PRINCIPAL

Progress

THE CREW   **THE SEASON**

Figure i.5

"*The economy has fundamentally changed. We've moved from a world with digital to a digital-first world; and there's no going back. Digital has become **the way** for people to connect, work, learn, and be entertained and the imperative for digital customer engagement has never been greater. Every business must understand their customers to deliver personalized digital experiences.*

"*The brands that win this race will have hands-on leaders who are open to change, a culture built around trust, rapid decision making and action, as well as a dedication to innovation and learning. Most of the evolution we have seen through*

COVID-19 has centred on transactional needs, be it the global pivot to online shopping or the rise of digital finance. However, brands must also consider how these unprecedented times affect people at the cultural and emotional level."

Paul Robson, President of Adobe International, Adobe

There are no silver bullets

If you have picked up this book hoping to find a silver bullet that will solve your business' problems, we're afraid we are going to disappoint you. Harmonising these three themes takes time, effort, and a great deal of motion. What we are sharing in these chapters, however, is aimed at helping you uncover how to translate your motion into progress and become a more adaptive organisation in the process.

Each part of this book covers topics related to that component of the business ecosystem. We begin in Part One with leadership, which comes from the principal. Without a clear direction of travel, you may meander aimlessly or go in circles, so setting that North Star is an important starting point. You also need to know how to measure your progress. Without clear measurement of the right metrics, you can't see how far (or not) you've gone and are therefore in danger of slipping back into a cycle of motion.

In Part Two, we move to your team and organisational ecosystem, including its culture. This component involves not only aligning your crew behind your vision, but also how you can support your team members to contribute to that progress, deliver on your goals, and do so in a way that draws on their strengths. Autonomy is one of the key concepts here, but this has to come with clear guidelines and a definitive North Star.

Finally, we explore the enterprise environment in Part Three, which is represented by the season. These are the events that you have to manage and adapt to as a business, but they are ones that are outside of your control. For example, the economy, political upheaval, global pandemics, and even the weather impact organisations of all sizes and in all sectors. This is not only about navigating challenges, but also about spotting opportunities and knowing when and how to take the shot that can significantly accelerate your progress.

Uncovering your starting point

You and your organisation are on your own personal journeys, with your own starting point. At the end of several of the chapters, we have provided a link to a series of online exercises that will help you to understand what stage you are at, what direction you may need to move in, what changes you may need to implement, and where you can find support.

Use these resources to help you apply the lessons from this book in your own business. Our aim is to help you understand how you can turn motion into progress, and to clear any rocking horses out of your boardroom.

Working towards meaningful transformation

We live in a world where competition really can come from anywhere, and businesses have to be able to rapidly respond to threats and adapt to change. Organisations must evolve multiple strategies and use these abilities to build and maintain persistent relationships with their customers. So, business transformation tends to be at the top of most large corporate agendas, to modernise businesses that have fallen behind in some way and need to rapidly play catchup.

In many cases, there is also a customer experience transformation (CXT) happening to meet the fast-shifting needs of customers, who today are empowered and in control. CXT is the combination of data transformation and digital transformation, which relates to a business' ability to respond in today's expectation economy. This is a world where customers are increasingly digitally savvy. They have choice. They are informed. They can and do vote with their feet (increasingly with their smartphones!). They expect service. They want quality. They are vocal when they don't get it.

If you are one of the many businesses that is transforming across multiple areas to make up lost ground, then this idea of building a business that can turn motion into meaningful progress will be very topical for you.

In our current work for Merkle and dentsu's Customer Experience Management service line, Rich as Chief Strategy Officer, EMEA, and Az as Chief Marketing Officer, EMEA, this is a topic we've tackled time and again with our clients. Over many years, we have seen and been part of extraordinary transformational efforts as well as attempts to transform businesses that did not gain sufficient traction.

What we are sharing in this book is a set of themes that any organisation can follow on its journey to becoming an adaptive organisation. Turning motion into progress is a key part of that journey. After all, how else are you going to get off the starting grid? However, as we're sure you know, making progress requires far more than simply turning on the engine and putting your foot to the floor.

The principles we share in each chapter are based on our experiences where we pull together examples and analogies to illustrate what we have found to be most important to a business' ability to become an adaptive organisation, and will hopefully provide you the guidance you need to harness that adaptive behaviour and turn it into meaningful progress. It is highly likely you already embrace at least some of them. However, if you are reading this book, there are also likely some obstacles in your path, some of which you may not even be aware of. Our hope is that you will find some ideas that can help you navigate those obstacles and continue your journey toward adaptiveness in the most efficient way possible.

If we help you overcome even one obstacle on your journey, we have achieved our goal. If you're ready, let's join the principal; it's race day.

Part One
Principal

Day is breaking over Silverstone race track on this July morning. It's the day of the British Grand Prix. The sun is shining and there are no clouds in sight, just as forecast. There is already a shimmer of a heat wave over the parts of the track that are being warmed by the sun's rays.

As the principal arrives at the track, they smile. They can go with their Plan A now that the conditions look fair.

Ahead of the race, the principal gathers their crew around them and gives them a final brief for the race. They explain the strategy, share any further information that they have gleaned from the reams of data generated during qualifying, and make sure everyone in their crew knows exactly what to do and when.

The principal talks with the lead race engineer and the driver separately. They are clear, concise, and focused. The goal is that chequered flag coming down on their driver. Everything they have done so far this weekend, and in the months leading up to this race, has been with this goal in mind. Throughout the season their strategy has evolved, taking each race as it comes, but there is always clarity over what the team is aiming for.

As the driver returns, suited up and ready to climb into their car, the principal takes a moment to soak up the scene. Everyone is in their place; everything is ready. The engine roars into life, the vibrations ripple through the air, and the smell of engine oil and fuel hangs heavy around the pit lane. The drivers start their slow procession to take up their positions on the grid, and the principal watches their car as it snakes along the track, warming up the tyres. A final glance around and a quick nod to the lead engineer shows the principal all they need to know: they're ready.

Every Formula 1 race team has a principal. This is the person who is responsible for communicating the team's vision and goals to the rest of the crew and leading for their constructor over the course of the race weekend, and indeed over the course of the entire Formula 1 season.

Principals set the direction for their respective team and clearly articulate the team's purpose, not only for each race, but across the season and indeed future seasons. They make sure that changes are made to the car to give the team the best chance of succeeding on race day. They oversee everything from the qualifiers that determine their starting position on the grid to the race itself. They set the strategy and make sure that this is communicated and executed by their crew, taking into account the external factors such as the track and conditions on race day. When there is an issue that affects operations, it is the principal who empowers the team, which will work to find the solution and chart a course out of any difficulties.

Being the team principal in Formula 1 is also an outward-facing role. Team principals will field many of the media's questions; they will take the criticism when the team doesn't perform as hoped; and they will also take the praise, although the best team principals make sure this is equally shared with the rest of the crew.

In addition to leading the way on race day, the principal is also the person who liaises with sponsors, hospitality, marketing, and many more. The principal joins all the dots to makes sure that the race crew can do its job to the best of its ability and present the team in the most positive light to the rest of the world.

There are clear parallels between being a principal and being a leader in any business. Within business, the principal is not just one person; a business can have multiple leaders at different levels in an organisation. In our context, the principal is any leader who defines direction or strategy. In the coming chapters, we're going to explore three key concepts that allow the leaders in any organisation to set the direction that the business will move in.

In Chapter 1, we look at the importance of selling the dream and vision, of clearly defining the purpose, and the importance of embedding that into a business' DNA from the start. Chapter 2 is all about measurement because creating the right measures is essential for driving the right behaviours and communicating the purpose that you're trying to achieve. You get what you measure, so you have to make sure that you're putting your focus in the right place. The final chapter in Part One is about prioritising your actions and making sure that you do the important things first. Don't try to boil the ocean.

All of these elements are a leader's responsibility, but we also want to be clear that when we talk about a leader, this doesn't have to just mean the leader of a company. It can be anyone who leads teams, leads on strategies, or provides thought leadership. Understanding the concepts we're exploring in Part One is important for leaders on every level within an organisation.

Leaders set the targets, but many businesses shoot for short-term targets because it is generally what shareholders want to see; however, this needs to be balanced with strategic focus on the bigger picture for longevity. This is all part of your culture; if you set short-term targets, people will have a short-term mindset. If you are only looking one step ahead of you as you walk, it's highly likely that you will walk towards a wall.

Focusing on the long-term goal, without breaking the journey into clear milestones to get there, is also far from ideal. If you are only focusing on the horizon, it's highly likely that you will fall down a hole. The key here is balance. Short-term targets are important to gain momentum and start to see progress. However, as we discuss in Chapter 1, you need to be able to keep one eye on this bigger picture to ensure your business and its programmes continuously evolve and adapt.

Chapter 1
The Peppered Moth
Why adaptation and evolution are essential in twenty-first-century business

"Being a fish out of water is tough, but that's how you evolve."

– Kumail Nanjiani

We'd like to begin by transporting you back to nineteenth-century England. The Industrial Revolution is taking hold, and the factories in the country's industrial heartlands are burning coal and pumping out black smoke. The residue from this smoke coats everything from buildings to trees.

Enter the peppered moth. In the 1800s, naturalists observed that peppered moths had evolved to fit in with this changed environment. The peppered moth is often found on the trunk of the silver birch tree and, therefore, its natural colouration is pale with darker spots, to match the colour of the tree's bark and camouflage it from predators. In highly industrialised areas of England, however, these moths were becoming darker in colour.

The pale-coloured moths stood out too much on the now-blackened bark of the trees and were therefore much easier for predators to spot. As a result, the pale moths were being eaten leaving the darker-coloured moths to survive and breed. Meanwhile, in regions where there was considerably less industrialisation the peppered moths remained pale in colour. They had no need to change their camouflage because their trees were not being darkened by soot.

This is probably one of the best documented stories of "adapt or die." Peppered moths in industrialised areas adapted and evolved because those that didn't died. It really was that simple. To this day, it's still widely considered to be one of the best examples of Darwinian evolutionary theory.

What does your business have in common with the humble peppered moth? It too has to adapt or it will die. In the business world, just as in nature, our environment is continuously changing and that means we can never stop adapting to match it. There are many organisations in the world today that are undergoing a period of transformation because they have fallen behind and they need to catch up. What we're talking about here is not only transforming to catch up, but making adaptation and evolution a core part of your business so that you never fall behind again (or ideally that you never fall behind in the first place).

As a leader, it is your responsibility to determine the vision, paint that picture, and state your organisation's purpose so that you never fall behind again. Think about the Formula 1 race team principal who is continuously evolving the team's strategy and car to make sure that the team stays ahead of the pack. The principal's driver knows exactly what has to be done on the track, the crew knows exactly what's expected of it before, during, and after the race. This clear direction is what allows all on that team to function to their best ability.

However, a Formula 1 season is never just one race. Depending on performance throughout the season, not only will there be pivots and changes to the strategy set by the principal, but the end destination might also change. A string of poor results might suddenly see your driver and team aiming for third in the championship, rather than first, or a series of exceptional wins could put your team on course for winning the championship, where your initial goal at the start of the season was a top-five finish.

The evolution mindset

3M is an American company that you might be familiar with and it perfectly encapsulates the evolution mindset that we're exploring in this chapter.[1]

In the 1970s, 3M used to be called Minnesota Mining and Manufacturing and at this time its scientists received a patent for the chemical formula that it was using to make masking tape, which had been in production since the 1950s. The story goes that the board was torn between whether to become a product company or a knowledge and know-how company.

If the board had chosen to become a product company, the company's product would have been masking tape. Of course, the company would have made different types, colours, and sizes of masking tape, but it would have pinned itself into a specific niche.

The board chose to go down the route of becoming a knowledge and know-how company, and 3M has since spawned over 60,000 products from that one chemical

(continued)

---

[1] Michel Robert *Strategy Pure and Simple II: How Winning Companies Dominate Their Competitors*, McGraw-Hill Education, 2nd edition (16 November 1997).

(continued)

formula. The core of 3M is that formula, and it has used that to continuously evolve and create new things.

Whether the board members recognised it at the time or not, they chose to go down a route of continuously adapting. They chose a process of continuous evolution. This is supported by the fact that 3M puts a material percentage of its turnover back into R&D and it encourages its employees to come up with new products and solutions. It empowers its people based on this core principle of adapting and evolving. It's an evolution mindset that starts at the top and filters all the way through the organisation.

The *Bandersnatch* process

In business, we have to pivot and change direction sometimes and it's important to remember that the destination we're striving for could also change depending on the route we follow. We also have to recognise that we are never going to reach that destination because that implies an end point. In business, there is no end, merely a constant evolution and adaptation to stay ahead of the competition. Just look at 3M.

The interactive film *Bandersnatch*, which was produced as part of the *Black Mirror* series for Netflix, is a simplified example of this process at work. As the viewer, you chose the direction the storyline took at various points throughout the film. In taking certain decisions around the plot, you influenced the ending that you saw. Unlike the world of business, *Bandersnatch* does of course have an end.

However, it illustrates the point about choosing your direction of travel well. Much like in real life, in *Bandersnatch* you don't know what ending you're heading towards when you start watching the film. Each decision you take for the main character leads you along a specific story arc. You're essentially opening a door and stepping through it without knowing what's on the other side, even if you might be able to predict what you expect to see.

Another key difference between *Bandersnatch* and business is that in *Bandersnatch* you can never go back. Once you take a decision about your direction of travel you are committed to that trajectory. In business, this might be true in some cases, but not in others. Often it will be possible to step back through a metaphorical door.

What we have to recognise in a business context is which doors we can leave open to step back through if we need to, and which ones close behind us, leaving us to navigate forward from that point. As a business, it's vital to make that distinction because if you're stepping through a door that will close behind you, you need to be confident of your next steps from there.

How can you tell if the door you're about to step through will stay ajar or close behind you? There are a few factors that will play a role here. The first is the speed at which you're travelling through that door, because if you race through really quickly, by the time you realise you want to go back, you might be too far from the door. The second is measurement, which we discuss in greater detail in Chapter 2, but fundamentally if you're measuring the right things you will be in a position to retrospectively change the elements that need changing.

Each business will be different and therefore whether it is able to go back through a door will vary. However, all leaders should be challenging themselves on these decisions. As a leader, what you have to work out is whether getting a particular decision wrong is reversible. If the answer to that question is "no", you have to take time to make that decision.

If the decision won't kill your business, you have to consider what the cost will be for you to step back through that door and course correct. The deciding factor should be whether the opportunity outweighs the risk of making the decision quickly.

Don't proxy process for performance

Picture the scene: You're in a meeting with a client pitching them an innovative solution that you've invented. It's going to cost your client £1 million per year to buy this solution, and they have estimated the opportunity cost for them will be £25 million. You know your solution is ahead of the market and, because it's not available through any other providers, you're confident as you walk through your pitch.

It's a slam-dunk . . . . Or is it?

There are many examples in business where process gets in the way of logic. Logically you would think that spending £1 million a year to gain £24 million is a no-brainer for a business of any size. However, here is an example of where this has played out in a global organisation.

A client firm was offered a solution to a specific business problem that was not available from any other provider at that time. However, the client firm was concerned that, because the solution wasn't available with any other providers, the firm might not be getting a fair deal. As part of its procurement process, the firm mandated the company pitching to go to tender for the project. Can you see where this is going?

Essentially this meant that the supplier had to facilitate competitors to pitch on its idea. Following the tender process, the client firm was concerned that the supplier might be £200 000 more expensive than the other options. Remember that the opportunity cost to the client was £25 million per year, and that the supplier had the solution ready to go. The client took two years to make a decision, at which point it chose the initial supplier, which was the organisation that pitched the idea in the first place.

The client lost £50 million in opportunity cost to make sure it wasn't spending £200 000 a year more than it should. Its process completely dominated logic. There is a good chance that if the client had paid the £1 million, it could have saved two years of time and taken a chunk of that £50 million in opportunity cost.

This story highlights the danger of allowing your process to dominate logic. We can all think of scenarios in which a business decision has been driven by process rather than by the opportunity that the decision carries. As businesses grow, they become more process-driven and they start to put each decision through the same process; whether it's for a £100 000 project or a £20 million project.

Sometimes you just have to let the logical solution take over and leave the processes behind. If a Formula 1 driver spots a gap in the race to jump up a few places to a pole position, the principal can't let that opportunity slip just because it's not on the race plan, but instead adapts the plan.

Emotional intelligence is more than a process

There is a lot of talk within businesses across all sectors about the need to have empathy. However, we believe that focusing only on empathy isn't enough. What businesses need instead is to focus on emotional intelligence. What's the difference?

Empathy often feels like a box that needs to be ticked. Are you empathetic with customers? Yes, good, job done. In some companies you can almost hear them saying, "If you want empathy, go down the corridor and it's the third door on the left." This misses the point.

Emotional intelligence (EQ), on the other hand, is much more about empowerment. Empathy is a part of that, but when you focus on emotional intelligence within your organisation, what you're doing is empowering people to think differently and giving them the authority to make decisions that are in the best interests of your customers and, therefore, your business.

Rich's take

Would you like a free coffee?

Pret a Manger is a great example of a company that allows and encourages its staff to use EQ when dealing with customers. It gives its customer-facing staff the authority to give away a certain amount of free product each week, but it doesn't specify who should receive that free product.

It's at staff members' discretion who they give those freebies to. I benefited from this policy when I used to buy a coffee from a Pret store near my office every morning. One of the baristas who worked there got to know me and, some days, she'd spot me at the back of the queue and nudge me to the front, hand me a free latte and I'd be on my way.

Now, I'm sure that in many instances the barista had mistakenly made a latte when someone ordered a cappuccino, so she had a spare latte and would give it to me. But she had the power to use that mistake to delight a regular customer.

Principles guide the business

The reason that having solid principles is so important is that you can't possibly map every single customer journey or interaction, or predict every single reason that a customer might get in touch with your business.

What you can do is embed a set of principles so deeply into your company that everyone knows how to respond in any situation in a way that matches your brand.

Rich's take

Can you help us improve, please?

I've been a customer with Harry's, which provides a razor blade subscription service, for some time, and at Christmas the company emailed me about a special edition razor it was offering. It wasn't expensive at £24, and for an extra £10 I had the option of having it engraved.

I thought an engraved razor would make a nice gift for my son, so I ordered one. When it arrived, my first thought was

(continued)

(continued)

that my order was wrong because all I could see was "Harry's" written on the top of the razor. Then I realised that my son's initials were engraved on the bottom of the handle, and the engraving was so faint I could barely read it.

It's fair to say I was disappointed, so I sent Harry's an email, explaining my issues with what I'd received. This was at 8 p.m. on a Thursday night. Very quickly, I received a reply from a lady who told me her name was Sunny. She apologised and told me that the money was already on its way back to my account. She also asked if I could take a photo of the engraving and send it to the company so that it could improve its engraving process.

Shortly after this exchange, I received another email asking me to rate Sunny out of five. I rated her five out of five. I then received another email that said: "Thanks for rating Sunny five out of five. What would you do for Sunny? Buy her a beer, give her a day off, or send her on a vacation?" All of this happened at 8 p.m. on a Thursday night for a £34 product.

Her response to my complaint was driven by the principles in that business because there is no way that she would have had a specific process to deal with a complaint about a faint engraving on one of the company's razors.

Compare and contrast that example about Harry's razors with another experience Rich had with a very different brand at a similar time. He wanted to test drive an £80 000 car from a luxury brand in preparation for an automotive presentation, so he contacted two dealers on a Sunday night to book his test drive. One dealer got in touch with him by lunchtime on Tuesday, and he's still waiting to hear from the other dealer he contacted.

That's a stark difference. Harry's solved a problem with a £34 product within minutes at 8 p.m. on a Thursday night, but a luxury brand, at best, took 1.5 days to respond to a request for a test drive and, at worst, didn't respond at all.

As a leader, selling the vision you have for your company goes hand in hand with embedding those core principles in the business. To get buy-in from not only everyone who works for you, but also your customers, you need to very clearly paint this vision from the outset. Without having clarity over this vision, you will also struggle to set the direction for the business.

"The best way I've found to open that aperture – without losing the focus – is to bring together a data-informed narrative that includes signals on brand relevance and saliency, consumer engagement, where consumer trends are going, along with quantitative marketing attribution (imperfect as it may be). Marketers are fundamentally storytellers, and it is incumbent upon us to shape a more nuanced story of what drives short- and longer-term brand success. Then, it's all about having a CEO and board who can take that in, and believe in it too."

*Marisa Thalberg, EVP, Chief Brand and
Marketing Officer, Lowe's*

Look at the 3M example that we shared earlier in this chapter. Board members clearly set the vision for the company when they decided to focus on knowledge rather than products. This key principle translates into cultural behaviours within the business that filter through to every person who works for and with you. In starting here, you're ingraining this behaviour and empowering your employees to start building a culture that reflects what you're trying to achieve. It's like a waterfall effect and it all starts from effective communication from leadership.

The aim is an adaptive organisation that can transform motion into progress

As a business, you might be working towards transforming your customer experience, but what we want to help you achieve is becoming an adaptive organisation. Why is that distinction important? Because there is no end. As we said earlier, this isn't a linear process with a final destination; it's a constant evolution.

The peppered moth that we talked about at the beginning of this chapter embodies that concept. Not only did the moths living in highly industrialised areas become darker in colour as their environment became polluted by the soot from factories, those same populations of moths have since returned to a lighter colour because a lot of the pollution that existed decades ago has been cleaned up. That species has continued to evolve to adapt to its current environment. A business is no different.

As a leader, you need to have a transformative mindset, which means that you're able to reframe your dream or vision for the business when required. Amazon's AWS service is a great example of this. It was initially developed as an internal system to manage Amazon's own infrastructure, but it quickly became clear that the technology had a multitude of applications that could be useful to a range of businesses. As a company, Amazon looked at AWS, recognised an opportunity to productise and monetise it, and then reframed what that meant for their business. Amazon adapted its offering and altered the direction of its business in the process.

Another way to look at this is through the analogy of buying someone a fishing rod versus teaching them how to fish. Imagine that each of the villages along a river represents a business. What often happens is that the people in one village look across the river and see that all the people in that other village are well fed. They look closer and see that they have fishing rods, so they go out and buy the same rods.

However, there is a difference between having the fishing rod and knowing where to find the fish, what bait to use, and how to start reeling them in when you do get a bite. Knowing how to fish is very different from having a fishing rod. What the people in that first village need to do is learn to fish, not buy fishing rods. Within business the same principle applies.

It can be easy to look at a competitor and think that if you have the same tools as it does, you'll get the same results, except this ignores all the knowledge that your competitor has. Our advice is to learn to fish instead of rushing to buy fishing rods, and our hope is that this book will help you to do that.

We often see businesses making this mistake in relation to technology: when an organisation will decide to change its technology because other businesses around it are doing the same. However, it's important to consider that changing your technology might not lead to the results you want. You have to ask whether you're using the technology you have correctly, how you can leverage what you've got, and whether you're driving the right value. Can you adapt how you're using your tools, rather than just throwing them out and buying new ones? Sometimes you will need new tools, but don't buy them because your competitors have them. Learn how to fish and decide if you need a rod or a net.

Progress accelerator

If you go to www.motionintoprogress.com, you can complete a simple online questionnaire that will help you frame your purpose and identify what direction you need to be heading in.

Highlights

The bottom line is that every business needs to continue to adapt and evolve throughout its life or it will die. You can no longer have and follow a single strategy; businesses need multiple strategies that they execute at the same time. To be able to execute multiple strategies simultaneously, and to do so effectively, you can't necessarily continue to work the way you always have; you need to continuously adapt.

Each organisation needs to focus on building and strengthening its change muscle so that adaptability is built in. One of the keys to successfully adapting is a leader's ability to clearly communicate that big picture, which sets the direction of travel for the whole organisation. We also have to keep in mind that there is no end to this process.

"It's never not day one" is a famous quote by Jeff Bezos. It comes from a letter that he wrote to his shareholders in 2017, 20 years after he started Amazon. In that letter he explained that there are four days in a company's life: day one when you're relevant, day two when you're in stasis, day three when you're irrelevant, and day four when you slide to death. He stated that his role as CEO of Amazon is to make sure that "It's never not day one." How do you make sure that you're always at day one? By adapting.

Chapter 2
The Chicken KPI
Focus on outcomes and progress will come

"One accurate measurement is worth a thousand expert opinions"

– Grace Hopper

To start this chapter, we're going to take you out for fried chicken. A chain of fried chicken restaurants has been working incredibly hard to improve efficiency across its many outlets in the US. One of the KPIs they have set for their managers is to have as little leftover chicken at the end of the day as possible.

A few months after introducing this KPI, the managers at head office are pouring over the figures and they notice that one of their restaurants is consistently reporting zero leftover chicken. Clearly the manager of this outlet has cracked the art of reducing waste food. "Can you imagine what this might mean if we can share this solution with our other restaurant managers?" one manager says.

A consultant who has been working on the efficiency drive is asked to travel to this fried chicken restaurant to learn the manager's secret. When he arrives, he's greeted by the manager who proudly shows him around the premises.

The consultant makes notes as they go, looking at the working practices of his employees and seeing very little that is different to what he's seen in countless other restaurants in recent months. As they sit with a coffee, the consultant asks the all important question, "The reason I've been sent is because your record on waste chicken is the best in the business … " The manager beams. "Everyone at head office wants to know your secret, because we very much want to share it with our other managers and locations," the consultant continues.

Still smiling, the manager replies, "It's really very simple; I just stop cooking chicken at 5pm every day, then it's always all sold by the time we close up." The consultant pauses, looking flabbergasted, "But aren't you open until 11pm at night?" he asks. The manager nods, "Yes."

"So what do you do if someone comes in at 8pm and asks for fried chicken?" the consultant asks, although he fears he already knows the answer. "I tell them that I can cook them some fresh," the manager replies. "Do they wait?" The manager shakes his head as he says, "No, usually they leave because it takes about half an hour."

The consultant has stopped writing. He knows this is definitely not the magic solution that those at head office were hoping for. He dreads to think how many customers this particular outlet has lost in recent months due to the manager's approach to reducing food waste.[1]

The moral of that story is that you have to be very careful what you measure, because you get what you measure. If you measure your outlets based on how much chicken they have left at the end of the day, they might have no leftovers, but you will also lose all the clients who come in after 6pm.

---

[1] Mark Brown, (2019), 'The Chicken KPI: Be Careful What You Measure', *Corporater*, 18 Feb 2019, available at: https://corporater.com/en/the-chicken-kpi-be-careful-of-what-you-measure/

The Healing Pyramid

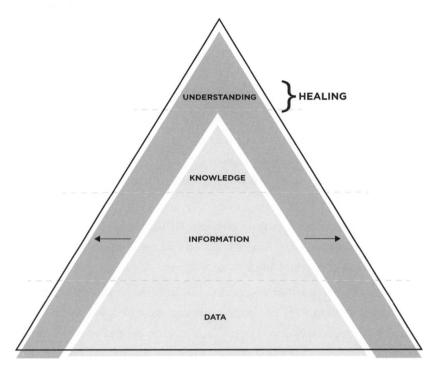

Figure 2.1

The Healing Pyramid was adopted by a medical researcher in South Africa who recognised that there was something missing from the traditional data, information, knowledge pyramid. You use data to create information, and you use information to drive knowledge, but this research recognised that you also need understanding to use that knowledge in the right way.

He explained this in the context of doctors and posed the question, why is it that, two years after a doctor gets 90% in their final exam, you can sit in their consulting room and watch as they struggle to diagnose the various symptoms of multiple sclerosis, even though they only studied it two years ago? It is because this knowledge is imparted outside the context of why they receive that knowledge; that is to say the understanding is missing. In this context, understanding is healing. His point is that if knowledge is imparted in a tertiary institution, outside the context of healing, those doctors don't learn to diagnose, they only recall knowledge they've learned.

In business this concept is incredibly important. If you put your business knowledge into the context of your organisation then you will be able to use that knowledge to solve problems that you didn't even realise you had solutions for, because you are starting from a place of understanding.

How does this relate to the chicken KPI story we just shared? That story is a demonstration of what can happen when you measure outside of that context of understanding.

To frame this another way, think about how you were taught times tables at school. If you're of a similar age to us, you probably learned by rote, so $2 \times 2 = 4$ and that's it. However, if you have kids, you may have seen that the way they now teach times tables is using a grid method because it breaks down multiplication to give children the understanding of why this works rather than teaching them to recall the answer.

When it comes to measurement in a business setting, you have to be able to contextualise the data you have and what that means for customer experience. If we take net promoter score (NPS) as an example, many businesses know that their customer satisfaction is lagging so they focus on increasing their NPS. They put in place all kinds of measures and religiously track their NPS and then celebrate when it increases from 7.6 to 7.7 for example. But if they can't contextualise what that actually means then what is the point?

What does that 0.1 point increase actually mean? Can you say whether that 0.1 point added X amount of revenue, saved X amount of clients or led to X amount of referrals? In the vast majority of cases, the answer is no. Too many organisations obsess about the measure, rather than what that measure is designed to bring, which in the case of NPS is improved customer experience, but what does this mean to the business? When you have understanding, you are able to bridge that gap, contextualise your knowledge and use it to make a material difference to your customers and therefore to your business.

A clear vision and purpose is essential to drive that understanding. In the last chapter we talked about the importance of the leader defining the vision and selling the dream. Like the principal of the Formula 1 race team, they set the direction of travel that the whole business is going to follow. Measurement is key, because without measuring what you're doing, you won't know whether you're progressing.

"Brands measure the past because it's much more comfortable. Trying to quantify the future and embrace trends when they are emerging is much riskier, but the reward is potentially much higher."

Paloma Azulay, Global Chief Brand Officer,
Restaurant Brands International

If you're not clear about what you should be measuring, you won't be able to track whether you're going in the right direction and moving towards your vision. As the chicken KPI story shows, if you measure the wrong metrics, you're going to move in the wrong direction.

In Formula 1 they measure everything to the nth detail. Look at the pit stop as an example. Not only does each team measure the overall length of their pit stop, which is defined by the length of time the car is stationary in the pit lane, but they also break this down into its constituent parts, measuring how long it takes to unscrew and screw on each individual bolt when changing the wheels, as well as how quickly the car is jacked up and lowered.

Beyond the pit stop itself, which has been reduced to under two seconds for all the top Formula 1 teams, they also measure pit lane time, which is the length of time their driver is in the pit lane. This contextualises their pit stop data, because having the fastest pit stop won't help you if your driver is in the pit lane itself for three seconds longer than your competitors. Time isn't the only metric that Formula 1 teams measure here either. They also measure the speed at which their driver enters the pit box, whether they hit their marks perfectly (and if doing so cost them any time), and many more.

Businesses can learn a great deal from the way in which Formula 1 teams approach measurement and how they use various data points to contextualise their overall performance. In Formula 1, measuring, understanding and contextualising even the smallest bit of data can be the difference between being a world champion team and going home empty handed, which is why every team in the sport invests so much to get the most out of every measurement.

Mistaking motion for progress

In the introduction, we talked about how rocking horses don't belong in boardrooms. Motion is very different to movement. In many cases, it can feel like Groundhog Day[2] where a

---

[2] *Groundhog Day,* (1993), Harold Ramis, Columbia Pictures

business goes through a wash, rinse, repeat cycle, doing the same things over and over again without getting anywhere.

To illustrate this, our friend Ben, who has worked for a large multinational organisation for 15 years, in a conversation recently, told us that he's really hoping a project he's working on at the moment will actually reach completion.

We dug a little deeper and discovered that in the entire time he's been with that organisation, not one of the 14 programmes he's been involved with has come to completion. Every programme has been vast in scale, and the organisation hasn't introduced the right measures to track progress. There is plenty of motion, they are rocking back and forth, but they aren't moving forwards at the pace that they could be to capitalise on their opportunity.

First things first

In the first chapter we talked about setting out your dream or vision. That's a vital first step, because any organisation needs to know what it's trying to achieve. You need to ensure that everything is pointing to the top of that mountain. We want to help you focus on what the top of that mountain looks like and visualise the views from the summit. This is setting a clear vision and purpose.

However, we also know that the thought of climbing that mountain can be daunting and it's not a task you're going to complete in one go. Once we know what we're aiming for, we can start to break that down into small, incremental steps to make the whole process easier to digest.

"Oftentimes people forget to start with the end in mind, working backwards to work out how to enable what they're aiming for. Take Disney, they didn't start by deciding to put bands on the wrists of everyone who visited their theme parks. They first realised that if they had data about where everybody was, how they were purchasing and how the flow in the park was moving, they would be able to improve certain elements of the customer experience. It was only when they understood how this could improve the customer experience that they went out and implemented the technology to do that.

The experience has to come first. Only once you understand what this looks like do you explore how to enable that experience and bring it to life."

Craig Dempster, Global CEO, Merkle

Focus on the outcome

As Jeff Bezos says, "Don't proxy process for performance." If you measure process, you'll get process. On the flip side, if you measure performance, you're more likely to get progress and move towards your vision.

Most businesses have too many projects. In addition, most businesses are geared up for starting projects, but they're not geared up for seeing them through. Be honest if this is an issue you can identify in your business. It's understandable because the traditional business process is centred around the business case and justifying the investment, but once that investment is approved, it becomes about tracking whether that investment is being spent on time and on target. What many organisations don't track is the outcome of that investment. Essentially they are measuring the process instead of what really matters: the result.

By bringing the focus back to the outcome, you gain clarity across the whole project and are able to ensure it moves forwards, rather than just moving with no real direction or clear purpose.

Not everything that matters can be measured

Albert Einstein once said, "Not everything you can measure matters, and not everything that matters can be measured," and therein lies the issue. Businesses measure what they can, but it's important to acknowledge it can be difficult to measure certain metrics.

As we've said, this measurement also needs to happen in the context of understanding. Budgets are a good example, because businesses often measure whether a budget was spent, rather than understanding what it was spent on and how, in the context of what they're trying to achieve, it will drive progress.

Rich's take

Bury the food …

I had my first lesson in budgeting during my compulsory military service in South Africa. I was on an instructors course in the South African bush with seven other men. Our food was delivered from the NCO camp and on the first night they arrived with three of the largest pots of food you have

(continued)

(continued)

ever seen. One of these pots would have fed 20 people, and we had three between the eight of us.

We didn't even get through one of these pots, so my Corporal turned to me and one of the other guys on the course and said, "Dig a hole and bury the food." I looked at him quizzically and he tapped his head while saying, "You idiot, if you don't bury it tonight then tomorrow night we'll get half as much!"

What I learned here is that you get what you measure, and in most businesses what is measured is whether a budget is spent, not how it was spent. Just like my army Corporal, those in most business departments know that if they don't spend all of their money then the following year they'll receive less, and they also know that they'll be lucky to ever get that budget back, so they focus on making sure it's all gone rather than on the outcome of that spending.

Whilst there may be a view of the initial outcome when the budget is created at the top, by the time it reaches individual departments, the original objective can often be misaligned to the expectations of what each team needs to achieve. Of course, whether a budget is spent isn't an indication of how well it was used, which is why organisations should consider how they measure outcomes connected to their budgets. Failing to measure these outcomes can result in budgets and targets being managed at a departmental level, missing the connected value that could be created.

These silos, caused by a failure to align measures, are a challenge in business. They are divided – it's right there in the name, you have different *divisions* of a business, from marketing, finance and accounting to sales, operations and logistics. Within a business, each of those is considered to be distinct. However, when you're trying to deliver for a customer it cuts across all of those divisions.

From a customer's point of view, they have purchased one logo, one brand. It's not their responsibility to know which division of a business they need to speak to, or to understand how departments are divided. Externally, the process needs to appear seamless.

Within a business, each division might measure what goes on in their part of the business, but seldom does anybody take ownership of and measure *across* divisions. There is no connection between the areas they can't control. There are no cross-functional ways of working embedded within the culture. When it comes to the customer experience in particular, we have to take a step back and ask what matters? What is the actual outcome we're trying to achieve across the whole business, rather than a result within a single department? We have to measure what matters.

"There is such a challenge getting all stakeholders / decision makers aligned on why the entire CX piece is as important as the numbers and why, when done well, it actually assists with driving the numbers in the right direction along with lots of other meaningful metrics like customer satisfaction."

Craig Smith, Decidable Global Ltd, Chief Brand Officer &
Co-Founder and Former Digital Commerce Director, Ted Baker

Rich's take

Misplaced focus

Growing up in South Africa, debt was expensive. Loan and mortgage rates were around 20% and although no one wants debt, many people had short-term loans. One of the largest banks in South Africa saw an opportunity here to boost takeup of its credit cards and started offering interest-free credit card deals for six months. As a result, many people closed their short-term loans and instead funded them through credit cards, taking advantage of that six-month interest-free period. As a consumer, you or I would probably do exactly the same. It's the smart thing to do.

Was it smart for the business though? The credit card sales team thought it was great. All of a sudden, they were smashing their targets and jetting off on all kinds of incentive trips. However, the short-term loan sales team saw their pipeline of customers evaporate. On an organisational level, all the bank had done was shift its customers from one silo to another, but in this new silo the customers weren't paying interest whereas previously they paid interest on their short-term loans.

This issue could likely have been foreseen and avoided with one simple change: measuring the profitability of the customer instead of measuring the performance of the individual sales teams. This decision almost halved the profitability of the average customer across these two business areas.

It sounds simple when you put it like this, but why is it that so many companies fail to consider projects across the whole business? The simple answer is because it isn't measured. American businessman Lou Gerstner once said, "People don't do what you expect, they do what you inspect." Most businesses inspect in silos, not across them. Just look at the story at the beginning of the chapter: if you measure the amount of chicken left at the end of the day, you get no chicken, but in that case you have to ask, what are you losing?

"Brands that are customer-centered were best positioned to adapt to the rapidly changing conditions caused by the pandemic, and generate brand growth and loyalty as a result. While we've continued to advertise to provide hope to job seekers, we've approached this time period with the mindset of prioritizing brand actions above brand advertising."

Jennifer Warren, VP Global Brand Marketing, Indeed

Another factor to consider is that most businesses measure what they know and habits form a part of this issue as well. When it comes to deciding what to measure, it's important to take a step back and ask that vital question, "How are we going to measure performance as a whole?" You have to look at what is already being measured within your teams or business and ask why you are tracking those metrics. Is it because they are important for helping you achieve your vision, or is it because you always have?

Savings, but at what cost?

If someone said to your business, "You can have £43 000 or you can have £2.4 million for your company, which figure do you want?" of course you would choose the £2.4 million. You'd be crazy not to.

However, as we all know, rarely in business is the question that clear-cut. We know of one company that, prior to being a client of ours, was working to save money on campaign efficiency. That is a very reasonable goal for a business to have.

This was in the days before online marketing had taken off and this particular organisation used a lot of direct mail, which is an expensive way to reach out to customers. Understandably, the business didn't want to mail people that they didn't think would respond, so they built a model with a lift curve, to predict who would be most likely to respond. That model revealed that 96% of their sales activity came from 80% of the people on their mailing list.

As a result, they decided not to mail that last 20%, thereby saving the business £43,000. On the face of it, that looks pretty good.

However, the reality is that although the response from that last 20% of customers was very low in comparison to the other 80%, it still accounted for £2.4 million in sales. They fell into the trap of focusing on the efficiency of their direct mail activities, rather than looking at the revenue that those activities drove.

It's another example of getting what you place your focus on, without realising this isn't necessarily the outcome you want. This particular business lost sight of the big picture and learned a painful lesson.

Connecting the dots

As we saw in the chicken KPI story, when you measure the wrong metric, you can get the wrong results. Often the reason an organisation is measuring the wrong metric is because there is a huge disconnect between the different divisions in the business.

Let's look at another example with a telecommunications company, where the aim was to optimise the website to increase handset sales. We're going to give you two scenarios in terms of measurement, as you're reading think about which would have the most positive outcome.

Scenario A: The main measure for the team tasked with improving sales of handsets is conversion rate. This is their key KPI and, under the contract with the company, they have a performance related incentive pay (PRIP) relationship. The team is doing really well at increasing the sales of handsets, to the point at which the company begins to run out of stock. This, understandably, has a negative effect on the customer experience. Their only option is to reduce their performance, and therefore see their remuneration take a hit, in order to ensure customer experience isn't impacted.

Scenario B: The team will be assessed on its performance on two key measures: conversion rate and customer satisfaction on receipt of the handset. As with Scenario A, they also have a PRIP relationship that's linked to these two KPIs. The team is doing really well at increasing the sales of handsets and they notice that there is likely to be a supply issue in the coming weeks due to high takeup of new handsets. They change their tactics accordingly, ensuring that every customer that orders and receives a handset has a good experience, while slowing sales of new handsets until they have a new supply of devices. Their remuneration isn't affected, because customers are satisfied with the service and when new handsets become available they are able to ramp up their sales activities again.

This is a great example of where businesses need to balance profitability with customer experience. Focusing on only profitability can lead to negative experiences. Focusing on only experience can lead to negative profitability. Empowering the crew to focus on both can lead to a positive outcome.

"Many brands hesitate to evolve what they measure, and how they measure it, simply because they are wary of what story might present itself. We often find this in the DEI space. Brands are excellent at putting out statements and presenting a picture of equity and inclusion, but when you look at the numbers—be it representation, pay equity, etc.—you see a different story. However, measurements drive accountability, and accountability is the only way brands will make real progress. Just look at how Salesforce closed their gender pay gap. They ran an audit for gender-based pay disparities, went public with their figures, and adjusted every single salary as needed. Many other companies have followed suit, but not enough. That's why the Female Quotient has become so focused on creating tools that close the gaps, helping organizations create a path for progress."

Shelley Zalis, CEO, The Female Quotient

There's an old African proverb: "If you want to go fast, travel alone. If you want to go far, travel together." Often what happens is that different business divisions work alone and don't communicate or consider the impact their activity might have on another division, like the example we shared earlier. When you completely disconnect departments, particularly those that have an impact on one another, you incentivise people to make the wrong decisions and do the wrong things – even if they appear to be for the right reasons.

You can see how this played out between the acquisition and retention teams we mentioned earlier, but this is a common issue within organisations across all industries. You see a similar issue when you look at retention teams, who are measured on how many customers they prevent from leaving, so all they do is give away products and reduce people's bills. What we want to do is join the dots. By making that connection across business silos, you can make sure that you're measuring what matters for the business as a whole, not just individual teams.

Az's take

Know your business model

In the mid-2000s I worked for a social media company that was going through its second round of funding. This was supposed to be the big one, where the business would get tens or even hundreds of millions in investment.

The company operated a social media platform, which was community-based and required people to join the site, build their own communities and websites, and then get others to join them as members or followers. Critical mass was absolutely key, so we were measuring the number of people who converted and registered to use the platform.

(continued)

(continued)

However, if I now tell you that all the revenue from the business came from people reusing and returning to the platform, would you say this was the right metric to be measuring? We operated an impression-based revenue platform. That meant if we didn't get enough people to come back, there was no revenue.

As you have no doubt deduced, we were mistakenly measuring conversion, without considering whether people came back. Unfortunately for us, often the people we converted didn't use the platform again which meant we were often converting the wrong people who we couldn't get back. Revenues were relatively flat, despite the fact that our conversions were up. This made the second funding round more challenging (although not impossible) for the business, because it was difficult to show growth momentum.

This just goes to show the importance of not only getting measurement right, but challenging what you think you should measure early on to ensure you really are putting your focus in the right place. It's a great example of proxying process for performance. We were measuring the process of conversion and had lost connection to the outcome that it drives.

Measurement as a catalyst for change

The key, and what we focus on in our work with all of our clients, is changing organisational structure so that the focus is no longer on channels and products but on teams of people who are measuring the right metrics.

These teams collaborate, they work together, they sit side by side and in doing so they solve problems for clients, whatever those problems might be. This puts the focus on whether you have met the needs of your customer, not whether the website or mobile app is working. This is all part of the evolution that we talked about in the last chapter, where organisations are becoming more agile, adaptive and have the ability to respond to markets that are never going to stop changing.

Adapt or die is a key concept for organisations in any industry to grasp. How do you make sure that your business is always adapting? By structuring it to enable it to be more agile and adaptive. Measurement plays an important role as a catalyst for change in the structure of your organisation and behaviours across teams.

When measurement works

We're sure you're familiar with online businesses that will buy your second-hand car via a process that is designed to make the transaction quick and easy. One such business has a huge share of the second-hand car market in the UK; in fact, around 50% of all second-hand cars go through their platform. The way this business, and those like it, operates is very simple. When you want to sell your car you put its registration into their website, answer a few questions about its condition and then they give you an estimated valuation as well as telling you the location of their nearest centre that you can drop the car off at.

When you take the car to the centre, they inspect it, either confirm or adjust the valuation and then agree to buy it from you. What often happened when you took your car for the

(continued)

(continued)

inspection was that the salesperson would point out defects that you hadn't mentioned in the online questionnaire and then reduce the price being offered for your car. This led to very poor customer experience scores and the company's sales started to fall.

To solve this issue, they took a very simple step: instead of paying their salespeople commission based on the value of the sale itself, they started paying them commission only if the customer scored their experience at more than seven out of 10. This meant there was no longer an incentive to look for every tiny dent and scratch on a car to haggle the price down, because the customer wouldn't be happy, and therefore as a salesperson you wouldn't get your commission.

With this simple shift in what they were measuring, the organisation drove alignment across their sales teams and changed their behaviour much more quickly than any business transformation project ever could have done. You really do get what you measure.

The telecommunications company that we described above also took a similar approach to improving its retention issues. It recognised that it had significant early life churn, which means customers sign up but then cancel within their 90-day cooling off period. To encourage its sales teams to focus on signing the right customers, it decided to only pay its call centres on successful new acquisitions if they were still a customer in month four. This changed their approach from a hard sell to a need-based sell, and sales volumes went down, but average customer tenure and customer profitability increased.

Does it make the "car" go faster?

When you measure the right metrics, you can make better and faster decisions for your business. This concept is illustrated really well in the film *Ford v Ferrari,* which tells the story of Ford's efforts to build a revolutionary race car that could beat a Ferrari in the 1966 Le Mans race.

Ford hired Carroll Shelby to create this car and he hired driver Ken Miles to support him in the project. Their process was to incrementally improve the car over time and the question they always asked was, "Did it make the car faster?" If the answer was yes, they kept it and if the answer was no, they didn't.

When you're talking about this concept in relation to race cars, it's easy to know what to measure: Did you go faster? Did your car cross the line first? However, within businesses it can be more challenging to discern what to measure, because each division is like one subset of the car's engine. How do you measure that one specific part to work out if it is actually making the car go faster? This comes right back to the vision, because each division needs to know what it's contributing to in order to find the right metrics to measure.

Always ask "Why?"

In 2009, Simon Sinek delivered a very engaging TED Talk[3] where he explained his model for inspirational leadership, which always starts with "Why". His model is very simple, it's just three nested circles with *why* at the centre, *how* in the next circle and *what* in the outer circle. Sinek explains that most businesses start with what they do

---

[3] Simon Sinek, (2009), 'How great leaders inspire action', *TED Talks,* September 2009, available at: https://www.ted.com/talks/simon_sinek_how_great_leaders_inspire_action

and they move inwards, explaining how and often forgetting about the why.

He uses Apple as an example of a company that communicates its why first. Their communication with their customers starts with, "Everything we do, we believe in challenging the status quo. We believe in thinking differently." That's their *why*. Then they move to the *how* with "The way we challenge the status quo is by making our products beautifully designed, simple to use and user friendly." Only then to they get to the *what*, "We just happen to make great computers." What he very succinctly explains is that it's much more engaging when you start with why you do what you do, rather than what you do. Every business talks about what they do, but what differentiates you from other companies in your space is why you do it.

Aviva is a great example of a company that has made an effort to shift away from being a product-centric organisation to a customer-centric organisation. They recognised that they needed to understand their customers better if they wanted to encourage them to hold multiple products with their organisation.

One very simple step they took was to pull their strategy and related measures together on a single slide. That slide appeared at the start of every presentation or proposal that they made and if the proposal didn't align with what they were trying to achieve based on that slide, the project was deprioritised accordingly.

Customer experience vs revenue

When a business makes a decision to focus on revenue rather than on the customer experience, it's important to ask just how much it will be compromising on. Is that really the only metric you want to focus on?

Az's take

Ready for takeoff

About 10 years ago, we booked a family holiday and were flying with a budget airline. At the time, our children were five and three years old. At the time of booking the flights, we didn't pay extra to make sure all of our seats would be together, because their website explicitly stated that children would always be seated with their parents.

When we arrived at the airport on the day of our flight, we were told that because the flight was fully booked they only had individual seats left available and we would all have to sit separately. Obviously we couldn't let our three-year-old and five-year-old sit on their own on a flight.

We had to go around to other people on the flight and ask if they would mind moving so that my wife and I could get seats with our children, which was horrible for us and disruptive to the other customers. All of this came about because this airline's KPI was focused purely on filling all of its seats. They gave no consideration to the fact that they were catering for people going on family holidays who might have young children.

It was a purely revenue-focused metric that completely forgot about the customer. It would be easy to argue that the purpose at this organisation was all about the numbers, rather than being about giving families and other travellers an enjoyable holiday. So, while the airline had a clear financial purpose, anyone that's ever flown with them will know that customer experience is not at the top of their priorities.

(continued)

(continued)

An example of the opposite approach can be seen in many private health organisations, which proactively support people of a certain age through measures like a free gym membership and proactive health checks, designed to reduce their risk of suffering various health conditions. Their aim is to have people attending medical appointments as infrequently as possible, which is aided by reducing the prevalence of ongoing health conditions like heart disease and diabetes.

By placing their focus on the outcome they want, which is a healthier population, the organisation has found ways to encourage people to lead healthier lives. This is where their purpose is enriched by understanding, which ultimately identifies the important measures. In this case, unlike most other businesses, they *don't* want to see their customers soon.

This particular airline differentiates itself purely on price and as a result it has compromised on every other definition of value. This example also ties in with what we discussed in the previous chapter in terms of empathy versus emotional intelligence. This business might put a tick in its empathy box, but what it actually needs is a process that enables its staff to act with emotional intelligence.

The KPI Tree

For modern businesses to stay abreast of the relentless progression of change requires so many areas of parallel activity, that it is extremely difficult to know just what to focus on, and when to make it a priority. Everything seems urgent, and with businesses generally very siloed, it is a real challenge to get to the measures that really matter. The ones that will align the business to the purpose and drive the change to get there.

You need a method to get to the real drivers of value for your business. The metrics that will change your outcomes and drive the business forward. Metrics that don't get obscured by the current business structures, cultural perceptions and misalignment, technology initiatives, global vs. local constructs, etc., but are relevant to all of them. A method that can get to what really matters and ensure the focus is on making them happen.

A method that can also help the business prioritise these metrics so you don't try and do everything at once, but also recognising that not all businesses, markets or brands are created equal, and so even if the same metrics are defined, how to change them could require very different priorities for different businesses.

On race day back at the track, all the many metrics the team records are connected to a live screen where multiple real-time scenarios can play out. If we pit our driver now, and put the hard tyres on, he will fall back to sixth place, but on fresher tyres he will be 1.3 seconds a lap faster and so looks to catch the leader with two laps to go. If the pit stop takes two seconds longer than planned, the driver comes out in eighth place. This means the settings on the car need to change to compensate for the extra speed now required to do an additional overtake and it's now going to need to happen on the last lap.

All of these metrics are connected, and they all are optimised to the final position on the track when the chequered flag comes down.

In most organisations, very few of the crucial metrics impacting overall value are truly connected. Many measures don't directly impact any outcome at all, and so the movement of them consumes time and motion, but can't be directly linked to any tangible outcome or progress.

This is where the multifunctional KPI tree comes in:

We use a mathematically connected KPI tree to solve these challenges. A logical process that unpacks the business objectives into a series of connected metrics and levers, and links the actions the business must take to move these performance levers (we developed a KPI tree for a multinational retailer turning over €34bn and there are fewer than 20 core levers that drive the business, so the focus is really on the levers that matter).

This tree can, of course, turn into a forest really quickly, but the logic of the process ensures that this doesn't happen, and the focus is put on actions that drive material value, in a prioritised way.

We have talked in this chapter about the importance of measuring what matters and using these measures to drive focus and alignment. This is only possible with the measures that really drive the business, and most of these will cut across silos and business functions and even geographies. Without some framework with which to do this, many businesses measure what they can, rather than what they should and so motion is often not translated into the progress that it should.

We have included a subset of this process to get you on your way (if this has resonated with you and you feel this is something your business lacks). It would not be possible to put our full KPI framework to work in this book (it is a complicated process and requires experienced facilitation) but the approach is logical, and we have created a sample of how this works to illustrate it for you. This should be enough detail to take you through how to get to the metrics that matter, but it is not intended to be a substitute for the full process.

Progress accelerator

To test the metrics you have at your organisation and learn how you can improve the metrics you're setting, use the KPI tree exercise on our website: www.motionintoprogress.com

Highlights

The key takeaway from this chapter is that you get what you measure. If you measure the right things, you'll drive the right behaviours which will result in a business that isn't just moving, but is making significant progress too.

As we said in the introduction to the book, rocking horses don't belong in boardrooms. You have to get away from mistaking motion for progress, because a rocking horse will move all day but it won't go anywhere. You have to turn that motion into progress and forward momentum. The way to do this is to make sure you're very clear about not only what you're measuring, but also that you're certain you're measuring the right metrics.

You get what you focus on, so by measuring the right metrics you direct the focus of everyone in your business to the right outcomes. Almost every business could probably benefit from questioning its metrics and asking *why* it measures certain things, and whether those really lead to the desired outcomes. As we've seen, measurement can be a powerful catalyst for behaviour change within businesses.

Leaders need to ensure that the metrics they measure tie in with their vision, but they also need to continually check that the metrics they are measuring are still the right ones as the business and the world evolves. Experience is the new battleground and that presents a multitude of challenges for businesses in terms of what and how to measure. Get measurement right, however, and you will go into the competitive battleground armed with a significant advantage.

Chapter 3
The Queen's Gambit
Translating strategy into tactics

"Strategy without tactics is the slowest route to victory. Tactics without strategy is the noise before defeat."

– Sun Tzu

The room is silent. You could hear a pin drop and there's a collective hush. In the centre of the space in a pool of light, two men sit at either side of a chessboard. All the perfectly carved black and white pieces are lined up neatly on the chequered board.

One of them is Magnus Carlsen, a Norwegian chess grandmaster who holds the record for the longest unbeaten run in classical chess and who is currently unbeaten in over two years of competitive play. His opponent is the relatively young Polish grandmaster Jan-Krzystof Duda.

The game begins with both men staring intently at the board and occasionally making notes as the game progresses. Each player takes pieces from his opponent, with both deliberating over their moves. As the number of pieces on the board decreases and the game edges closer to a conclusion, you can feel the tension in the air. Eventually, Duda has it and Carlsen faces his first defeat in 125 games.

Even with all of his experience, knowledge, and foresight, Carlsen was beaten by a relatively junior chess player in professional terms. This just goes to show that, despite being masterful at turning strategy into tactics, things can come out of left field and surprise even the most seasoned and experienced of us.

Chess grandmasters can hold more than 20 potential future moves in their head, but they don't ever consider more than four to six moves ahead because they don't know what their opponent is going to do. They know that there's no point in thinking 24 moves ahead because their opponent's response is going to change what they do. They always have to respond to the opposition.

Within chess there are already many, many options; and each of those options comes with more options. When you factor in what your opponent does, this adds a further layer of complexity to those variations.

However, a regular chessboard is two-dimensional, which means that you can see everything that's happening. You have a view of the whole board and can begin to map out your strategy, even if you know that might need to be altered based on what your opponent does. For businesses, the reality is more like the game of three-dimensional chess that appears in *Star Trek*.

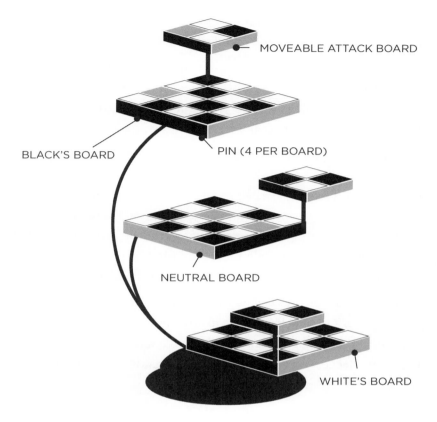

Figure 3.1

This board has multiple levels, some of which are moveable.
If you look at it from above, it looks very similar to a standard chessboard, but you can't plan your strategy in this game by only looking
down on it. You are playing across different levels; you can move certain platforms depending on the strategy you're following, and so can
your opponent. You have to look at the board from multiple angles;
a piece on level one can still take a piece on level three, for instance.

Adding this third dimension brings yet more complexity to the game, even though you are fundamentally still following the rules of chess.

Playing three-dimensional chess is therefore closer to how businesses operate in the modern world. There is an element of unknown, you might not be able to see everything at once and you may have to test the waters at times to make sure you're covering all bases.

Thirty or 40 years ago, being in business was more akin to playing traditional chess. Many businesses were fairly one dimensional in that they would set out a strategy and follow it. In the modern world, with new technology, and customer habits and preferences evolving, businesses need multiple strategies. Those strategies need to be tested simultaneously, which we talk more about in Chapter 4, and you need to be in a position to rapidly course correct when necessary.

In business, you are playing chess in multiple dimensions and you can't afford to play from the top any more. You'll have multiple strategies and be making decisions that have short-, medium-, and long-term effects, so it becomes harder and harder to know what to do next.

If you're going to do something, do the *right* thing

In the previous two chapters we've talked about the importance of having that big vision and purpose for an organisation, and how measuring the right metrics can ensure everyone is aligned on how to achieve that vision. In this chapter we're going to look at the importance of doing the right thing and not jumping to conclusions about what that right thing is.

But what is the right thing? There isn't a single answer to this question, but as Jeff Bezos says, a good place to start is customer obsession. Making the shift from positioning products in the minds of customers to being relevant in the lives of customers is the key.

"Brands today are seeking ways to drive desirability and engagement, which ultimately leads to conversion and sales by putting technology and programs that connect directly with consumers at the forefront. By putting consumers at the heart of what we do, consumers will respond positively."

Doug Jensen, SVP – GTM & COE for Analytics & Activation,
Estée Lauder

Focusing on outcomes over outputs

Many businesses focus on outputs rather than outcomes. Outputs are deliverables that don't necessarily add inherent value, such as a presentation or a piece of functionality on your website. Outcomes are tangible results that have a measurable effect on a business goal. The problem with focusing on outputs is that it doesn't necessarily move you any closer to achieving your vision. You're back to sitting on your rocking horse thinking that you're going somewhere because there is motion when, in reality, you're still in the same spot.

When you're trying to solve any problem, it's therefore important to focus on the outcome rather than the output you see. This involves considering multiple strategies with multiple outcomes to find the right one in any given situation. There are multiple routes to your outcome, the key is in deciding and prioritising which you are going to take.

Think of this journey a little bit like the challenge from the game show *Takeshi's Castle* where you have to run to the top of the hill while dodging boulders. Just like in business, you have your North Star (in this case the top of the hill), and just like in business, there are multiple ways to get there.

Where you hide, how you climb the hill, and the route you take might vary, but your ultimate aim will be to reach the top of the hill. You have to be agile and flexible when it comes to choosing your route: Some of the routes will be shorter; some will be longer, but result in fewer hits from boulders rolling down the hill; however, whichever route you take you are still moving in the same direction and orienting yourself by your North Star.

In *Takeshi's Castle*, there is another game where contestants have to run through a series of doors to reach the end of the course. Some of the doors will be blocked, some of them will be clear, and some of them will have people behind them who then chase you. Contestants have to make very quick decisions or they will end up off the course and in the water. In business, it is really no different.

You need to be able to run through doors quickly, taking advantage of the ones that are clear, but course correcting rapidly when you face an obstacle. Agility is key when it comes to making those decisions, which means moving away from a linear approach to decision making and being prepared to quickly change direction if you go through the wrong door.

Learn and evolve

Amazon Dash is a good example of how you can test and evolve an offering as a business. Initially the service was designed to allow you to order certain products for your home quickly and easily when you needed them. The basic concept was that you would have a button that was connected to your Wi-Fi, and you kept this button in the cupboard next to your cat food, for instance.

When you ran out of cat food, you could press the button and more would be delivered to your home the following day. The problem was that the smallest container of cat food you could buy from Amazon was two months' worth, which defeated the whole object of the system.

We suspect that Amazon Dash didn't take off as a service for consumers for that very reason. However, Amazon took the engine that drove the Dash product and embedded that in devices like Kyocera printers. It's now called Amazon Dash Replenishment (a little less catchy), and if you have a printer with this product, it will automatically order you new ink when it senses that your ink is running low.

With its Dash buttons, Amazon was testing its customers' appetite for wanting to replace certain products on short demand. While the buttons didn't work, the company learned from it, pivoted, and as a result has created a new service that is performing significantly better than the Dash buttons. They ran through a metaphorical door, got an undesirable outcome, but instead of falling into the water they used their agility to pivot and end up with a much better result for the business.

Yesterday's tactics aren't tomorrow's strategy

In the past, there was more focus on personal selling, that is one-to-one between a customer and sales representative, and it was focused on the customer's need. Today, selling has become much more focused on personalisation. However, this isn't focused on customer need; instead it is about selling to people at every available opportunity and selling to people via channels rather than one-to-one. We see the future strategy for businesses being more personal as the battleground for customer experience grows.

There is an evolution happening here, which starts with what we call next best offer (NBO). This is where, as a business, you create a range of offers you think your customers want, based on what you know about them, and the next time you encounter them on a particular channel, you present them with that offer, irrespective of what that customer actually wants. In this instance, the business is doing something to the customer.

The next step in this evolution is next best action (NBA). Rather than simply selling, this involves a business thinking about what action a customer might take next. You create a range of customer journeys, drop your customer into one of those journeys based on what they're doing, and try to nudge them along that path towards what you want them to do. This is also an example of doing something to the customer.

Finally, we have next best experience (NBX). This is where, as a business, you see a customer has a need, you try to understand what that need is, and you curate what that moment needs to look like to meet that need. When you do this as a business, you are creating experiences based on what each customer needs at a specific moment in time.

However, many businesses still base their decision making around selling, which leads to what we consider a very one-dimensional approach. There is a significant focus on being personal and the commoditisation of data, which is all centred on selling and giving customers the next best offer, rather than the next best experience.

Experience is the next battleground for businesses, but we're not talking about experience simply in terms of how an app performs or how someone serves a customer. We are talking about the entire experience a customer has with an organisation or brand. Next best offer is just one subset of that experience. The whole experience battleground is considerably broader, and includes the three main stages we previously talked about, the first of which is next best offer.

"As professionals who pride ourselves on our ability to connect with people, we rarely speak of the customer experience in terms of trust and values. It's one thing to understand audience data and behaviour, but the COVID-19 pandemic has rightfully brought trust to the top of boardroom agendas alongside ROI and conversion rates. In particular, brands are looking at new ways to deliver personalised digital experiences that establish trust with their customers.

"In practical terms, this realisation has inspired a shift in mindset for brands. Where the early days of personalisation were about serving up relevant offers and deals, the practice has now evolved to cover every element of the customer journey."

Paul Robson, President of Adobe International, Adobe

This is an evolution, with each step increasing in complexity as you go.

Next best offer (NBO): We would equate the next best offer to a Rubik's cube. From any starting position, the cube can be solved in a maximum of 20 moves. There are a limited number of ways it can be mixed to give you a starting position, and a limited number of ways to solve it.

A step up from next best offer is next best action, which is where you start thinking about the next action you want your customer to take, which isn't necessarily limited to just buying a product or service.

Next best action (NBA): To continue our gaming analogy, we equate next best action to a game of chess, where there are 400 possible options after the first two moves have been taken. While this is still a finite number, it is considerably more than 20 and introduces greater complexity to the decision-making process.

However, what leading businesses are starting to lean towards is delivering the next best experience. This is where you ask, "What is the next experience I think this customer wants?" It results in a much more personal experience for each customer, which is tailored around emotional intelligence (EQ) and understanding that customer's need.

Next best experience (NBX): Within games, this is the equivalent of playing Go, a Chinese strategy game that has been in existence for more than 2,500 years. After the first two moves in Go there are 130,000 options. While still finite, this is a much closer comparison to the unlimited nature of human experiences than chess or a Rubik's cube.

4_{30} 10_{123} 10_{360}

Figure 3.2

Experiences are created from many moments where customers interact with brands. These moments don't all neatly connect into the customer journeys that we expect them to take. We can't plan for every eventuality because the journeys are complex and we don't always know what customers will want next.

Not everything is in your control

If you think about the game Go and how many options open up after those first two moves, you can see how the complexity of the environment you're operating in increases significantly. You can't control what moves your opponent will make, and you therefore can't completely control the direction the game takes, although you can steer it through your own moves.

When you start thinking about NBX, the options are vast. There will also be a number of factors that come into play that set outside of what you know about your customers. It's no longer as simple as looking at their browsing and purchasing history on your site to present them with similar products.

To develop a better understanding of what NBX could be for any given customer, it helps to consider the three ways in which you interact with customers: outbound, inbound, and unbound.

Outbound interactions are the ones you're fully in control of. These are communications you send out to the customer, so you're in control of the timing of that communication as well as what it contains.

Inbound interactions are the ones you receive from your customers. These are on the customers' terms and therefore can sometimes present a challenge because you won't always know when you're going to receive these or what they will contain. Sometimes it's possible to force an inbound interaction by asking customers to respond, at other times it will be a case of your business responding to whatever customers send to you. These are the interactions that significantly increase the complexity of next best experience.

Unbound interactions are the trickiest to manage because they are the elements that you as a business are unaware of and generally not in control of, but that may still have an impact on your journey with customers and their overall experience.

A good example of this is when a customer applies for a mortgage with a bank. The bank can only control so much of that customer's experience, because a customer will also be working with a mortgage broker, a solicitor, an estate agent, a surveyor, and possibly others. There are many different factors that aren't necessarily part of your journey as a brand, but that can still affect the overall experience that customer has.

What can you, as a business, do to handle all these possible permutations of a situation and still provide the next best experience for your customers? The best way to deal with this is to create a framework that is able to flex according to the myriad customer reactions you may encounter as well as those unbound interactions. Adaptability needs to be baked into every aspect of your business.

Immersive versus invisible experiences

We think of two categories of customer experiences that you, as a business, need to be aware of: immersive experiences and invisible experiences. Immersive experiences are the ones everyone sees. We all know when a brand does things to delight its customers and we're aware of them happening to us when we are a customer.

Invisible experiences, on the other hand, are the parts of a brand's offering that simply have to work, and as a customer we shouldn't necessarily be conscious of them. There is often limited measurable benefit to getting an invisible experience right, but it can come with a very costly consequence when you get it wrong. A great example is broadband – the only time you notice it is when it's not working. However, it is important to understand what the customer needs regardless of whether you are delivering an immersive or an invisible experience.

Many organisations fall into the trap of doing something cool and glossy because it is cool and glossy, rather than considering whether that particular activity meets a customer need. The key is to begin by identifying the need among your customers, and then deliver an immersive or invisible experience accordingly. You should be able to draw a line back from every experience you offer to the customer's needs that it meets.

Just like every single component of a winning Formula 1 team is deliberately designed for maximum performance, everything you design in your customer experience needs to be deliberately designed to match up with the customer's needs. Paying attention to these intricate details is what is going to produce memorable moments that add up to experiences that your customer values.

Az's take

Are you sitting comfortably?

When my wife and I moved a number of years ago, we decided to buy a new sofa. We simply needed a temporary sofa for our house, which meant that I wanted one at a reasonable price. I was, however, aware that if my wife and I visited a store, she would likely choose the most expensive sofa going. I did hours of research across all the main sofa manufacturers in the UK and one of the ones I was seriously considering was a sofa offered by one of the UK's largest sofa companies.

(continued)

(continued)

There were three main things that I, as the customer, was looking for at that point in my journey: Did the sofa meet my budget? Would the sofa fit in the space I had in my living room? And would the colour match? I looked at the same parts of that product page over and over again, and at no point during my dozens of visits to the website did the business make that experience personal to me in a way that would have taken my encounter to the next level.

Now, the company website was trying to get me to go into one of their brick-and-mortar stores because the company knows that its conversion rate goes up as soon as a salesperson gets involved. However, on my particular journey, I didn't necessarily want to go to the store. In fact, buying online was the better option for me, given that I was concerned my wife would choose a much more expensive sofa if we went into a physical store! However, it didn't allow me to convert online, and the result was that I purchased my new sofa somewhere else.

Had the company considered alternative customer journeys and experiences, it might have been able to adapt to meet my needs as the customer, which in turn would have resulted in me purchasing one of their sofas. It's a good example of a business trying to facilitate a particular experience, but hasn't considered whether it's an experience the customer actually wants to have.

There are also nuances around the definition of a personal experience. Amazon is a company that provides its customers with a very personalised experience, but it does so in a very impersonal way with no emotional attachment. These subtle nuances in how you can approach the concept of NBX can make it very challenging to know where to begin as a brand.

"The answer is 42"

If you've read *The Hitchhiker's Guide to the Galaxy* by Douglas Adams, you'll know that 42 is the answer at the end of the book to "the ultimate question of life, the universe, and everything." However, in the book the question wasn't defined and therefore those seeking it needed to build an even more advanced supercomputer (the Earth) to find the question. The irony, of course, is that Earth is destroyed just before it is about to reveal the question.

If your plan is to turn motion into progress, it's a good idea to start with the question. Many businesses start with the answer and work backwards to find the question or the root of the problem. If we look at Amazon, it starts with the question: "How do I make a customer happy?" so it always starts at this point and works towards the answer. Because this is so ingrained in the business, certain things, such as refunds when a customer complains, happen automatically. This brand value drives certain behaviours and outcomes.

Finding clarity through classification

We started the first chapter by talking about the peppered moth, and we're going to return to a zoological example now. If you look at the fields of zoology and botany, there are millions of species of plants and animals on this planet. Yet every single one of them can be put into a complicated classification system through simple diagnosis.

This classification system has many layers, so you can move from a species to a family to a class to a kingdom. As a business, you have to find a way to classify the needs of your consumers to make that information more digestible. When you can do this, you're suddenly not trying to make a decision based on a million possibilities. You are classifying the challenges, and in doing so you're able to determine the ones that are irreversible from the ones that can be changed through a similar classification framework.

Having this clarity reduces the risk of making the wrong decision because you better understand the challenge and you know the solution you are working towards. You have a defined direction of travel.

Of course, having a defined direction of travel can reduce your room to manoeuvre, and this is particularly the case when you carve out a niche in a very specific area. The challenge in this instance is how do you diversify and change your trajectory without unwinding much of what you've already done? The key lies in this classification system.

How do classification systems aid decision making?

The classification system you have at your business will empower (or if you get it wrong, disempower) people to deal with your customers in an intelligent way. To illustrate how this works, we're going to look at how a stealth bomber manages to stay in the air because according to the laws of aviation, it shouldn't.

We've even heard these planes described as having the aerodynamics of a shoe being thrown across the room. So, how do they stay in the air? The answer is the computer systems that carry out a multitude of micro adjustments every second. The pilot of a stealth bomber therefore doesn't actually fly the plane because a human isn't capable of responding to that number of decisions so quickly.

The pilot is still steering the plane and managing the weapons and communications systems, but if that plane gets into trouble then it ejects the pilot to preserve his or her life and self-destructs to protect its secrets from falling into enemy hands.

Working in a customer-facing role these days is a lot like piloting a stealth bomber, except you aren't in a position to eject and self-destruct if you get into trouble. Every customer interaction could lead to myriad situations and that means people are faced with making myriad decisions every day.

If there aren't enough, or the right, systems in place to empower the people in those customer-facing roles to make the right decisions, they're trapped in a restrictive process, much like a pilot would be in a stealth bomber if they didn't have the option of ejecting. Having a classification system can help your employees in customer-facing roles to digest and distill the millions of options in terms of how they could react and guide them towards a response that meets a particular customer's need.

This is moving towards augmented intelligence, where a business uses machine learning to provide insights to its team, which can then make informed decisions to deliver better services to customers.

When we're dealing with people, we have to respond in an emotionally intelligent way. Having a clearly defined classification system within your business allows your customer-facing people to do just that.

Although the leader of an organisation won't necessarily be involved in creating these classification systems, they will set the principles that overlay the classification hierarchy. These principles will encompass what the company thinks about its customers as well as what it does and doesn't want to do for its customers. A business' principles have to be deeply embedded within its DNA so that everyone who works for that company understands them and can act on them.

Az's take

Give good solutions

As customers, Rich and I tend to be very tuned into what we experience with different businesses. I recently ordered a T-shirt online and although it said it was in stock when I placed my order, on the same day a customer service rep from the company got in touch to tell me that it was no longer in stock.

He apologised and acknowledged that it was the company's mistake. Then he gave me three options:

1. You can choose anything you like from the online store to have as a replacement, even if it's more expensive (bearing in mind this was just a £25 T-shirt).

2. You can wait for the T-shirt you ordered to come back into stock, which will be in about two weeks.

3. You can have a refund today.

I ended up changing the T-shirt I had ordered to a different one, but the company also sent me a voucher for money off my next order, which meant I then bought something else. The principle at work here was clearly to give customers good solutions to any problem and to do that quickly.

Now compare that to another experience Az had where the principle to make the customer happy was not nearly as deeply ingrained as the principle to make the business money or save time and costs.

Az's take

No onions please

My family went out for a meal with friends to a pizza chain and one of our friends ordered a pizza with no onions because she has an intolerance to them. When the pizza arrived, there were onions on it, so we called the waitress over, explained that she had an intolerance to onion and would get a bad reaction, and we sent the pizza back.

The waitress apologised and took the pizza back to the kitchen. A short while later, she returned with a new pizza for our friend. Except it wasn't a new pizza, it was the same pizza we'd sent back, the chef had simply picked the onion off it. You could still see the impressions of the pieces in the cheese!

This tells you a lot about that business' brand values. The company wasn't concerned with customer safety (it's lucky our friend has an intolerance and not an allergy), and it wasn't thinking about making us happy. The company were thinking about saving money for the business and its bottom line, although it did offer to remove the drinks from our bill by way of an apology.

It costs around £1.50 to make a new pizza so the right thing to do would, of course, have been to just make a new pizza without onions on it. This is where businesses need a flexible system to guide human (or chatbot) behaviours for this to be effective.

It is also why it's so important to clearly define your brand values and then use them to drive every interaction with a customer.

Don't jump to conclusions about what the answer is, instead you start with identifying your problem and work to find the right solution to solve it.

The Moment Builder

"To connect deeply with an audience, you need to create a more equitable relationship and be willing to give up some control. Let people take the lead and be willing to have a conversation that is authentic. Let people decide when and where they want to make transactions and on what terms. Follow people rather than expecting them to follow you and build experiences for what people want to do, not just what your brand is looking to achieve."

Nicola Mendelsohn, CBE, VP GBG, Meta

To effectively provide an experience, we've discussed that you need to be able to adapt at speed. The actions that you take are underpinned by everyone in the organisation making the right decisions that make a difference to your customer at the right time. This means that you need to shift from curating experiences and waiting for the right time to deliver them, to having a system through which to curate an appropriate response to any moment. Curating moments will give brands the opportunity to better respond to their customers' needs and build meaningful experiences as a result. To do this requires a classification system.

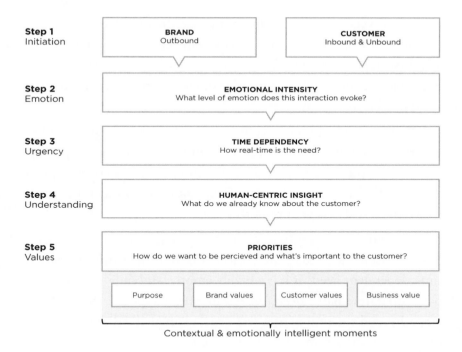

Figure 3.3

A system is made up of a hierarchy of layers, which can evaluate any customer moment to produce the right response, even if it's just a one-of-a-kind situation.

These layers can be multifaceted and very complex, and what we have illustrated in the preceding diagram is a simple representation of what this might look like in our Moment Builder. Let's step through it and see how it is used to understand moments that matter to your customer.

Each step seeks to understand the context of whatever moment is in question and quickly curate an appropriate response.

In this version of the Moment Builder, the first step would establish if the moment is initiated by your brand or your customer. This first step is important because there may be a material difference when responding to a proactive brand intervention versus an incoming customer engagement.

Now you can add the level of emotional intensity that might be experienced by the customer as a result of this interaction (step two). This allows you to lay out the degree of empathy that may be required to deal with this interaction in the most meaningful way possible, which in turn affects your response.

You can then step into level three, urgency. Here you can assess how real-time the need of this customer is. In other words, is there a time-dependent need? If it is a highly emotive, inbound interaction, based on a time-based need, the nature of the response, the level of empathy, and the timing of it will be fundamentally different to a non-emotive, non-time-dependent moment.

For example, a car rental company responding to a phone call of a customer who has broken down in one of its vehicles is going to elicit a very different level of response compared to an email from a potential customer.

These types of (illustrative) dimensions begin to underpin what you know about the state of this given moment.

The last two layers in this example then start to define how you curate an appropriate experience for that moment, using what you know about your customers, what they value, what they care about, and their experience with the brand. These are human-centric insights that you can use to contextually frame the right response. For example:

1. **What values does the brand want to be known for?** Do you want to be seen as caring, sustainable, customer-first, or honest, for example?

2. **What do you think your customer values?** What do you think or know that your customer cares about? Convenience, price, or loyalty, for instance?

3. **What state do you think your customer is in?** What need do you think your customer is trying to satisfy and how can you use what you think you know about this customer to shape how you personalise that moment for him or her?

4. **What is the value of the customer to you?** There are some customers who bring more value to a business than others. In some cases, it may be that you as a brand need to step away from a particular customer, but you have to consider how to do this in a sensitive way, especially if one of the values you want to be known for is customer-first.

5. **What do you know about your customer?** What information have you consolidated? What is your customer's motivation and do you understand his or her emotional state?

Each of these parameters can impact how you respond to a given moment. In terms of the preceding point 4, let's take an online footwear and clothing retailer as an example. There could be two customers who order 30 pairs of shoes each, so on the face of it they both look like valuable customers. However, customer A returns 29 of his 30 pairs of shoes, whereas customer B returns 5 of her orders. With this added perspective, customer B is a lot more valuable to the business than customer A.

This retailer might reach a point where it needs to politely decline customer A, and it would use its values as a parameter to do that in the most diplomatic way possible so that it doesn't damage the brand or the business and still maintains a memorable customer experience. This is also where EQ would come into play.

As a business, you have to set the variables and parameters that make up the framework of customer experiences. The experiences you offer customers need to be based on responses to those rules, which then also allows you to factor in those unbound interactions that you as a brand don't have control over.

A good analogy to demonstrate how introducing these rules helps your business comes from tennis. Think of the umpire in a tennis match as the brand, and the players as the customers. In the past, when a ball was hit close to the line, the umpire would have the final say on whether it was in or out. The players would often argue and there might be a debate on court, but ultimately what the umpire said stood and there was no definitive answer in those marginal calls.

In more recent years, Hawk-Eye has been introduced to the professional game and this has removed all the subjectivity over whether a shot is in or out of the court. In addition, there are rules relating to how often a player can use Hawk-Eye to challenge a call by a line judge or the umpire in order to prevent players from abusing the system.

In a business, these rules give everyone who works for you a definitive guide on how to deal with different situations, so customers will get the same level of experience regardless of who they are in contact with in your business. Introducing additional layers of rules (such as how often tennis players can use Hawk-Eye) enables the business to quantify the experience and use it to guide the response to customers.

These principles have to be considered alongside a customer's value, however. If we go back to tennis, John McEnroe was famous for his shouting matches with umpires over their decisions, and he might seem like the kind of difficult customer you want to manage out of your business. However, at the peak of his career, the sport would have lost more by letting him go than it would have gained.

Much like the example of a footwear and clothing retailer we gave earlier, it's important to look at the value a customer brings to your business and discern whether he or she is worth hanging on to or whether this customer needs to be managed out of your customer base in a sensitive way.

"You've only reached your goal when customer needs are fully satisfied – and when they keep coming back for more from your brand. So, in that sense, it is a continuous learning process, always striving to serve customers even better than last time."

Benjamin Braun, CMO, Samsung

Rich's take

We're sorry your branch is closing

Managing a customer out of your customer base diplomatically and in line with your brand values can be done, but it requires a careful and well-thought-through approach. Years ago, I used to support the branch location function for a bank I worked for, and at this time we were closing bank branches.

(continued)

(continued)

We were sending our customers a letter letting them know that their branch was closing and what they could do next. Before we carried out a mass direct mail campaign, we ran a test and sent a small number of customers one of two letters.

The first letter read: "We're sorry your branch is closing. Here are the other branches in your area that are staying open. Please choose any one of them to move your account to and go and meet the manager." We only retained 60% of the customers who received this letter.

The second letter read: "We're sorry your branch is closing. We have moved your account to this branch, the branch manager's name is Sheila and here are some available times for you to meet her." We retained 90% of the customers who received this letter.

After this test, we knew the second letter was the best one to send to our customers. However, we also had some customers who we weren't keen to retain, so we sent those customers the first letter, knowing that we would lose around 40% of them, and used this process to achieve our goal in a constructive way.

This is an excellent example of how you can make hard decisions with your customers in a very diplomatic way while still living up to your brand values and choosing the direction you want to go in.

Rich's take

Cooking up a storm

In my house, we get a fresh meal subscription delivery three days each week and I do all of the cooking with these meal boxes because our entire family loves the food. One evening as I was unpacking the box and preparing to make dinner, I realised the gnocchi that was part of the recipe hadn't been included. I went into the company's app and found the chat option.

I explained my gnocchi was missing and the immediate response I had was, "We're really sorry, we'll credit £8 back to your account." However, that response didn't make me happy because while I have £8 in my account, I'm about to cook a meal and I have no gnocchi, so it doesn't really help me. After all, mushroom gnocchi without the gnocchi is just mushrooms!

I went back to my cooking and then I actually found the gnocchi in the box. So, I went back to the app and back into the chat function where I got another person (or chatbot) and explained that I'd just been refunded £8 because I thought I was missing the gnocchi, but that now I had found it I didn't need that £8 back.

The reply was, "We're terribly sorry this has happened, we've put another £17 back into your account." By this point I've been refunded £25 and I'm trying to explain that I don't want that money back.

It looks like the policy is to always refund a customer if they complain, don't argue with them. However, there's

(continued)

(continued)

no EQ applied in this scenario, and it appears that the rule is repeated if a customer gets in touch again; just give more money back. This could quite easily get out of hand for the business and won't necessarily help the customer either.

Any rules you set around your brand values and how you manage customer experience need to include EQ, or give your team space to use its EQ, and they need to be carefully managed. Your classification systems are what keeps this focused on customer's needs whilst being financially practical.

Do you remember the example Rich shared earlier about his experiences with the razor and shaving company Harry's? This was one step up from the fresh meal subscription in that the customer service rep at Harry's not only refunded the money immediately, but provided that human engagement that made the customer (in this case Rich) feel valued.

Another similar example came our way through a colleague, who placed an order with Beauty Kitchen, a sustainable and natural beauty products company. She ordered one of its sample sets to try out the products in its range before committing to buying larger pots of its products. When the sample set arrived, one of the samples was missing.

She emailed Beauty Kitchen and received a reply the same day apologising and promising to post the missing item immediately. Two days later, she received the missing product, along with some free samples and a voucher for 10% off her next purchase. Two years later, she tells us she is still ordering from the company because it responded with EQ to the issue she had with her first order.

Az's take

Product over people

I order hair products from a small business that makes excellent products; however, its service can be a little slow. There was one order I placed where the product had gone out of stock by the time the company was getting ready to send it out to me. The company contacted me to let me know this and, at this stage, I realised that I had made a mistake with my order and wanted to change the product I'd initially chosen for a different one in its range.

I emailed the company and asked if I could make the switch, but the reply I received said that it couldn't do this within its system.

The company could have quite easily switched out my product and sent me the one I actually wanted straight away. Instead, I had to wait a few days for the product I'd initially ordered to come back into stock before I could even arrange to change it. It felt as though the company's process was all about stock management rather than customer service, which is a shame because the company's product is excellent but its service doesn't quite measure up, which meant that I didn't receive a total customer experience.

Every sale matters

We have talked a lot about businesses that rely on repeat custom, but what about if purchases are more likely to be one-off transactions? In this case, it's even more important to get everything right because if you're just making one sale and having that one series of interactions with a customer, a bad experience really stands out. By contrast, if someone makes 300 purchases from you and only one of those goes wrong, the bad experience is offset by all the good ones.

Kat, a friend of ours, shared a good example of how to get this right recently. Around her birthday, her sister-in-law told her to expect a delivery by 1 p.m. the following day. Kat didn't know this, but it was a box of cupcakes. She stayed in all morning and by about 2 p.m. nothing had arrived, so she sent her sister-in-law a text just to let her know.

Her sister-in-law had received a notification that the order had been delivered, so she got in touch with the company to ask what had happened. The company immediately apologised and said it would send a new box of cupcakes for delivery the following day.

The second box of cupcakes arrived to Kat as promised, and it was all sorted. But this isn't where the story ends. A couple of days later, Kat's sister-in-law received an email from the cupcake company. It explained that, after she had contacted them about the missing cupcakes, the company received an email from a woman who said, "I think you delivered some cupcakes to me by mistake. I'm really sorry because I ate them but I felt guilty because I have no idea who Kat is and I thought you should know."

Even though the company solved the problem of the missing order quickly, it still had the EQ to realise that Kat and her sister-in-law might like to know what happened and why the cupcakes hadn't arrived. The company made it personal, which makes the customer feel valued and shows a human touch that is often missing when the blanket response to any issue is simply to provide a refund.

Making transactions personal isn't the only way to make customers feel valued when they are making a one-off purchase with you. How your business responds to any issues is just as important, even if they aren't your fault. Applying EQ in such situations can help you deliver an exceptional customer experience. It all comes back to thinking about what customers need in a given scenario and working out how best to deliver that for them and your business.

Rich's take

It's not our fault but ...

For my wife's 50th, I bought her a case of wine and I printed individual labels for each of the bottles using an online service. Now, both my son and I checked the labels, but both of us missed the fact that we had got her birth year wrong.

I had ordered 24 labels (double the number I needed, just in case), and all of them were incorrect, which was entirely my mistake. I got in touch with the company to ask if it still had my image on file would they mind amending the birth year and reprinting them, obviously at my expense. The response I received was that it would reprint them free of charge, as long as I cut up the incorrect labels and sent the company a photo to prove they had been destroyed.

It was wholly unexpected but another example of how, even for a one-off purchase, you can really elevate the customer experience.

From automation to augmented intelligence

The number of touchpoints between a business and its customers has increased significantly, while the range of technology to help organisations manage those customer interactions has also expanded and developed. As a result, businesses are seeking ways to make their inter-actions with customers smoother and more efficient, which is why automation is such a hot topic.

This technology undoubtedly has a place in the modern customer experience environment; however, it's essential that EQ is considered alongside automation, otherwise it can have the opposite outcome to the one you are intending.

We see many businesses turning to automation as one of their strategies to help solve problems along the customer journey and to try to improve the customer experience. However, it doesn't always work because it lacks that all-important component of EQ.

What businesses need to move towards is more augmented intel-ligence rather than automation alone. This involves interlacing the human element into automation to ensure that EQ is applied when it's required to not only provide a better customer experience, but to ensure that you don't inadvertently provide a poor customer experi-ence as a result of your automations.

Rich's take

Are your debts mounting up?

I've been with my bank for 20 years and I'm at a stage in my life now where I've cleared my mortgage and I don't have debt. I recently received a letter from the bank and the opening paragraph was, "When you're struggling to pay multiple bills and your debts are mounting up, sometimes it can put you at ease to know that your bank's got your back." Then the letter goes on to give me an example of how it would look if I borrowed a certain amount of money from them at 6% interest.

I know that in one of my other accounts I have more than the amount in the example, and it's currently earning 0% interest. The bank hasn't looked at my individual circumstances as a customer and thought to tell me how it can help me get more than 0% on my savings. It has just sent me an automated letter about loans.

That letter tells me everything the bank doesn't know about me and shows a complete lack of thought in terms of what it is sending to its customers.

This example also comes back to the disconnection between departments that we discussed in Chapter 2. It is particularly common in larger, legacy businesses like banks. Each department isn't considering the whole customer experience, it is only considering the part of the experience that it is responsible for (and sometimes not even doing that very well).

"The last decade was about the joy of metrics, an exuberance of progress in our desire for understanding. With so much more understanding of what tools we have and what we can measure. This decade is a refocus on informed insights and consumer connection. It's a journey for all industries that continues to move us forward and create more incredible experiences for our customers."

Deborah Wahl, Global CMO, General Motors

When a business starts to automate, and to do so at scale, it has to put classification systems in place for those automations to work. However, as we have explained, you can't automate for every situation and every customer. A one-size-fits-all approach doesn't work.

What we are seeing emerge is the need for a framework, based around your brand values, that allows for flexibility in how every person in your business deals with customers. In having this framework, you're encouraging each person within your business to ask: "What am I trying to say to this customer? What do they mean to me? What are my values?" And then each person applies the answers to those questions in a way that aligns with your brand values.

The point with this is that every message that reaches a customer will have gone through the same system, the same framework, to ensure it aligns with those brand values and that it brings value to the customer, whether it comes from the marketing department, the finance department, the sales department, or the customer service department, any interaction with the customer will echo those brand values.

"Customer expectations of convenience, simplicity, choice, and transparency have been set by digital-first businesses. Often, the biggest barrier for legacy businesses is their success to date – success built on decades of optimising a business model."

Nick Ratcliffe, Customer Experience Director,
Volkswagen Group Ltd

Although small businesses typically have fewer silos than large organisations, they can still fall into the trap of taking a blanket approach with their automations. Even if small businesses are able to avoid this initially, once they reach a certain critical mass the same problem is likely to appear. If you don't set out these frameworks as a foundation, at some point any business will run into the challenge of automating and scaling this.

Small businesses should consider these pitfalls in the early stages of their development because having this framework and rules in place will make it easier for them to send more tailored communications and have personal interactions with their customers not only now, but also as they grow.

Look at Amazon; it doesn't care about what particular type of customer you are when you make a complaint. It simply refunds because its core brand value is "happy customers."

It's never just one dimension

Automation is just one strategy that businesses can use, just as segmentation is a subset of one of the main dimensions each business needs to consider to deliver NBX. Think back to the example we shared at the beginning of this chapter about the three-dimensional chess game in *Star Trek*. When you are playing in three dimensions, traditional moves aren't as relevant and you need to consider the board and game from multiple angles. You can't afford to only take a top-down view or you risk missing important facts and information that will inform and improve your strategies.

In a similar way, for every customer interaction, businesses need to consider:

• What do we know about you? This helps curate the message specifically for that customer.

- What do you value? What the customer values in a brand further tailors this message.

- What is your need? We have to know what each customer needs to ensure what we're offering is relevant.

- What is the urgency of your need? This is particularly important because in some circumstances urgency will be the highest priority. If you're stuck at the side of the road trying to find out whether your insurance policy gives you breakdown coverage, the urgency of that situation is significantly greater than what segment you fall into.

- What part of the situation drives the emotion? Will the solution you're offering the customer calm their emotion? Think back to the meal subscription service example Rich shared earlier; if someone is trying to cook dinner one evening and he doesn't have all the ingredients he needs, being given some money back might be nice, but it's unlikely to calm his emotion.

Many businesses dive straight into finding a solution, which comes back to the concept of outputs versus outcomes. There's a physical deliverable from an automation programme (output), at the end of the segmentation process you are left with a segmentation model (output).

If you haven't taken the time to think about your brand values and prioritise which you need to implement and how you need to execute them, you will keep coming up with outputs rather than outcomes. It's outcomes that deliver business value.

It can also lead to a misplaced focus because sometimes the solution isn't always what you immediately think it will be.

Please don't leave your rubbish

There's a school in our area that had a real problem with people leaving rubbish by one of its fences because of the convenience of the space. Every time it happened, the school would have to clear it and it was getting fed up. So the school put up a sign that read: "Please don't leave your rubbish here."

A week later, there were more bags of rubbish by the fence. The school cleared them and then put up a new sign that read: "Please don't leave your rubbish here, offenders will be prosecuted."

A week later, there were more bags of rubbish by the fence. The school yet again cleared the rubbish, but then took some time to think about what the problem actually was. They updated the sign again, this time providing directions to the local dump, which was just around the corner.

With the new sign, no more rubbish appeared by the fence after the last collection of bags was cleared.

The school recognised that the issue was that people didn't know what to do with their rubbish other than to leave it there. They could see the sign telling them not to leave it by the fence, but in the absence of any other instruction they didn't know what else to do so they would dump their rubbish by the school. Once they had directions to a better option (the dump) they took it.

The solution to that problem wasn't as simple as the school initially thought, in terms of putting up a sign just telling people not to leave their rubbish there. By providing a sign explaining where the dump is, they gave people clear direction and steered them to the NBA.

The Fluid Cube

If experience is the next battleground, businesses need to think carefully about how they can deliver the best possible experience for their customers.

Consumers are not just one dimensional, and as a brand it's important to consider the many dimensions of each consumer and to be aware that those dimensions can change during an interaction. To help explain this concept, we've come up with the Fluid Cube.

Picture a Rubik's cube and imagine that this is the consumer. The various combinations and permutations you can arrive at when you mix that cube represent the consumer at any given moment in time. There are three different dimensions in terms of the fluidity in which consumers behave.

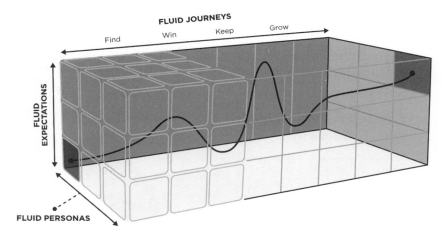

Figure 3.4

Fluid personas

People can move between personas or, in fact, be multiple personas at once. This means the traditional concept of personas and segmentation is often outdated. For example, Az and his son both play ice hockey. When he's shopping for gear for his son, he's looking for products that are going to protect him on the ice. The focus is on safety and health. When Az is shopping for gear for himself, he's looking for the glossy, shiny, sexy gear that's going to make him look good when he steps out onto the ice. He's still the same person, but the context changes.

Fluid journeys

This is about understanding the triggers that will let you know what the intent is for an individual customer. For example, if you look at a motoring website, how does that brand know whether you're looking for a second car or you want to book a service for your current car? Sometimes businesses can make the wrong assumptions about a customer's intent and that sends them down the wrong route.

If we go back to the motoring website, most of those businesses know that using a car configurator is one of the highest converters for booking a test drive (at least it was pre-COVID). As a result, most of those websites will push you towards their car configurator, but that doesn't account for an existing customer whose intent is to book a service. This could see that customer being pushed down the wrong route on the website.

Just like with personas, a customer can flip between journeys at any given moment in time and brands have to consider how they can start to mix that accordingly.

Fluid expectations

This involves thinking about each customer's expectations and intent, as well as their state of happiness. Think about the difference between NBO, NBA, and NBX. If a customer isn't happy with the service currently being offered, don't try to sell something else. Instead think about what the NBA is for the right level of service or experience that the customer should have next. In some cases, that might be nothing at all, such as a cooling off period.

The point is you have to account for whatever that next action is in some shape or form, instead of just trying to sell. Factor in the level of emotion and the emotional state of each customer in comparison to all the other dimensions as well and remember that this is a fluid process. Each customer will always be shifting and changing. This is why we developed the Moment Builder. You can't pre-create every combination of the fluid cube because it's fluid. You have to curate the experiences in the moment.

Highlights

As we noted at the beginning of this chapter, doing something isn't the same as doing the right thing. All three of the chapters in the Principal part of this book are fundamentally about alignment, and ensuring that every piece of your brand and business is moving in the same direction, that you're all part of the same metaphorical race and share a common purpose.

"The hardest part of the organisational journey that businesses have to go through, and indeed the hardest part of business in general, is that it is the organisation that gets in the way of opportunity. You need to have a culture that has a willingness to change, and if that culture isn't present, any efforts to transform will struggle."

Margaret Wagner, EMEA President, Merkle

Establishing a culture that is open to change is a key component in your work to become an adaptive organisation. As we move into the next part of the book, Crew, we're going to focus on autonomy and making sure that everyone in your organisation is empowered to be able to do the right thing. This is about creating a culture that enables change, ensuring that your organisation is not getting in the way of your opportunities.

We've started to touch on this topic already with discussions around frameworks that enable people to act with EQ and make decisions that meet the customer's need while aligning with the brand's values.

Let's come back to our Formula 1 team principal. They will start any race weekend by setting a clear vision for the team so that all know exactly what they are aiming for. The principal is making sure that everyone's focus is in the right place and that this is the right thing to be doing. And the principal will evolve their strategy over the course of a race weekend as it progresses to make sure that the team is still doing the right thing and making the right calls.

Then the principal will oversee what is happening with their car, their team, and their competitors to inform and evolve their strategy. Measuring the right metrics allows them to make alterations in the right places, and this is what gives them the edge.

Finally, the principal knows that there are many variables that can affect the outcome on race day, not all of these will be within their control and they aren't necessarily going to be available to make every tiny decision that's required to progress towards that vision. The principal will introduce processes and frameworks that every member of their team can work within to give them the greatest chance of success.

In Formula 1, this is complex enough; in the world of modern business, there are infinitely more variables and moving parts.

Understanding the complexity of the modern business environment is key. If you try to do everything at once, you won't progress. You have to make sure you are really good at one thing and if you focus on excelling in that area, you will see progress.

The key is working on your strengths as well as your weaknesses. Look at the difference in the quality of tennis players between the UK and the US in the 1990s. Each country took a very different approach to player development, and it was clear which produced a higher volume of top-ranked players. In the UK, players with a strong forehand but a weak backhand would be encouraged to focus on their weaker shot and bring it up to the same level as their strongest shot.

In the US, players would focus on making their strongest shot even stronger. In doing so, US players were able to excel far beyond their competitors. This brings us full circle to the peppered moth. When an evolution works, focus on what's working. Adapt or die, but if you adapt from a place of strength, you put yourself on a much stronger footing to not only survive, but to potentially thrive.

Regardless of how well you performed last year, without constant measuring, refining, and adapting, keeping up in a rapidly changing world is going to be an impossible task. The Formula 1 team principal understands this and inspires his crew members to improve their chance of success year after year.

The same applies to the world of business too if we are prepared to understand the need for change, can define measures that track our progress, and pivot according to the fluid movement of the marketplace.

Part Two
The Crew

Crew members for the different Formula 1 teams begin to arrive at the track. They too can see that conditions are near-perfect. The smell of fuel and engine oil hangs heavy around the pit lane. The morning is punctuated by the occasional roar of an engine and the sound of tools and parts being moved into position. There's a gentle babble of conversation and an electric excitement in the air that always accompanies a race day.

As the crews assemble, they get to work quickly and efficiently. Some are making final checks to the cars themselves, others are poring over data gathered during qualifying, making final tweaks to enhance performance by the smallest of margins. Just like the cars they are preparing, they are a well-oiled machine.

The principal moves among them, directing some individually and, as the start of the race nears, calls everyone together for a team briefing. As the cars leave the pit lane to line up on the grid, every member of the crew is in position. The team members are focused and know exactly what they have to do over the coming couple of hours. They all know that the aim is a win at Silverstone.

The roar of the engines mingles with the shouts of the crowd as the cars complete their warm-up lap. With all the cars in position on the grid, there is almost a collective intake of breath. The crew seems to pause as the noise dies down. Even those unable to see the lights at the start line know when the race begins, thanks to the deafening roar of 40 engines firing to life. The drivers are off, and every member of the crew is laser-focused on their role. They know what they have to do and how they have to do it.

Within a business, the crew encompasses a number of different things. The team is, of course, a crucial part of that and one of the most vital elements to understand is how to create momentum throughout the whole business. But the crew also includes the car itself and how you can tinker with it to improve its performance as well as the facilities and components you have available. In Formula 1, these are the elements that will allow you to shave fractions of a second off the time your driver spends in the pit lane or the speed of a lap.

All of these elements are things that a Formula 1 team can control. In business, the elements that are within your control equate to not only your team, but also the culture you create within your organisation. They also include the facilities you have at your disposal. In Chapter 4, we're going to start to tie together the leadership that comes from the principal and the crew. While the principal's role is to set out the priorities, when it comes to the crew, it's all about how you can move quickly as part of that process.

Think of a rocket that is waiting to take off. There is significant initial inertia when that rocket takes off because it has to go from a standing start to upward movement to get it off the ground. This often starts slowly, but then quickly gathers speed. What we are going to explore in Chapter 4 is how you can minimise the amount of time it takes to build up speed.

It's also important to bear in mind that, given the incredible force that's required to get the rocket off the ground, you are moving in the right direction once you have exerted all of that effort. This is why starting with the principals, who set the direction of travel, is absolutely key. However, once the principals have set that direction, they will need help to move, and this is where the crew comes in.

The energy that's expended to launch a rocket, or get a transformation within a business moving, is huge. That energy also won't last forever, so you have to ensure that you're using it in the most efficient way and at the right time. Think of a cheetah that's hunting on the plains in Africa. It can run incredibly fast, but only for a short period before it becomes exhausted. When it decides to sprint, it has to go for the kill, otherwise it doesn't eat that day. In business, this concept translates to making every shot count.

Chapter 4

Make Every Shot Count

Why agile decision making is essential to making progress

"Consider everything an experiment."

– Corita Kent

W e're transporting you to the late seventeenth century. The white sand palm-fringed beaches of the Caribbean might look idyllic, but to make a journey across the turquoise waters offshore you had to run the gauntlet of pirate ships as you transported cargo from one island to another.

Battles on the high seas were brutal and challenging. Unlike land battles, both your ship and the one you were fighting were constantly moving. Holding steady to let off a volley of cannon fire was no mean feat. Sometimes you had to fire one cannon to check the trajectory of your shot and course correct as necessary. Other times you could learn from the shots your enemy fired over your bow.

These battles required both pirates and merchants to adapt their strategies, learn, and evolve. There might be days where your boat was smaller and lighter than your opponent's, in which case you might decide to run and live to fight another day. On other occasions, you may be low on ammunition and therefore it becomes imperative to make every shot count.

To outsiders, it might even have looked as though you were firing in the wrong direction if you started firing before your enemy's boat had come around. However, your knowledge of the seas and how your enemy's ship was moving might mean that you hit your mark despite outward appearances.

As Sun Tzu said, "No battle plan survives first contact with the enemy." The point isn't that you shouldn't bother with a plan, but simply that you have to understand that you can't create one plan to cover multiple strategies and you can't plan for everything.

Instead, you have to know your capabilities and what your army (crew) can do; you have to understand the capabilities of the enemy (your competition); and if you expect them to attack from the right but they come from the left, then you just have to fight, adapt, and use what you know about your strengths and their weaknesses to help you. You have to go into battle ready to fight, but you also have to go into battle ready to adapt.

The battlefield of modern business

Businesses today don't have the luxury of following one strategy, as we explained in Chapter 3. The market is changing too fast and at a pace that it has never moved at before. As a result, businesses need to have multiple strategies and they have to be testing them all the time.

Jeff Bezos sums it up perfectly with the quote: "The faster we test, the faster we fail, the faster we learn", but while failing fast to learn fast is important, it's equally important that you don't fail in the wrong areas, otherwise your business won't survive to learn from its mistakes. You have to be flexible, you have to be quick, you have to fire your shots, and learn from them, but you also have to be watching what's happening in the environment around you and what your competitors are doing to make sure you are in a position to course correct when you need to.

It's also key to be able to separate the things that will kill you from the things you can learn from, so that you can avoid the shots that will sink your efforts. You also have to be able to pivot and evolve as a result of the shots you can learn from.

You have to have a flexible plan, be constantly listening to your customers and their needs, and feeding that back into what you're doing. You pivot, adapt, and course correct using that data.

There is one more element to consider, which is how long you should stick to your plan before you accept it isn't working and change what you're doing. As former heavyweight boxing champion Mike Tyson once said, "Everybody's got a plan until they get punched in the face." In boxing, your plan might not come to fruition until the fourth or fifth round of a bout, so you might have to endure several rounds of being punched in the face. In business, this comes back to the concept of learn and evolve. Take feedback, know how much pain you can take, and check your direction of travel to ensure you are still on the right path. If that one punch is going to knock you out, or in the case of a business seriously impair your organisation, you have to change your plan pretty quickly.

Many businesses will ask for a three-year plan, but what they actually need is a three-year vision and a three-month plan. Much like the chess grandmasters we talked about in Chapter 3, even though you might be able to see 28 moves ahead, you're not going to plan that far ahead because the moves your opponent makes will change your strategy.

As a business, you should think in terms of actions instead of in terms of years. Rather than planning out the next five years, instead plan the next five actions. You will still have your overarching vision guiding your direction of travel, but you are focusing on what actions you need to take, and that you can plan for in the short term, to help you move forwards.

"At General Motors, our vision of an all-electric future challenges us to define that future for, and with, our customers. We are on a journey together to solve their needs, enhance their experience, and create meaningful value."

Deborah Wahl, Global CMO, General Motors

This links back to what we discussed in Part One about the principal setting the direction of travel, but it's not enough for the principal to just set this direction, you have to communicate that to everyone in the crew so that you all know where you're heading. You will fire some shots, you will watch where they land, you will listen, learn, adapt, and course correct when you need to.

When you course correct, most businesses will follow the process of "ready, aim, fire," and you should take the "aim" and "fire" steps very seriously before you take that next shot to make sure that every shot counts. In this chapter, we're going to share nine principles with you that will help you ensure every shot counts at your organisation.

#1 Think big, start small, scale fast

This means that you can see the full picture. You and everyone else who is part of the crew understands the vision and your organisation's direction of travel. This big picture includes not only the crew, but your competitors, and if we return to our Formula 1 analogy, also the car, the track, and the weather. If you're a member of the pit crew, for example, your job might be to change the right rear tyre during a pit stop, but you will still know that the reason you're doing this quickly is to win the race and win the season. Your individual task is connected to the outcome.

This visibility of the big picture means that every person and element of the crew is connected and working together. There is no point in the pit crew members who are changing the tyres rushing to do it in two seconds if the person who is refuelling the car takes ten seconds to do her job. There's no point in getting one element right but getting the others wrong. In a business, that simply results in a disjointed experience for the customer.

Rich's take

Time to cool off

I recently cancelled my broadband subscription with a provider I had been using for years to move to a different company. However, I quickly realised this was a mistake and decided to go back to my original provider. By the time I contacted the company to move back, it had already cancelled my subscription.

(continued)

(continued)

When I phoned the company to explain the situation, a representative told me that there was a 10-day cooling off period, during which the new homeowner has to give permission for you to keep the telephone number. I said, "Well, that's fantastic, as I'm the homeowner, I give permission." The response I received was, "I'm sorry, sir, there's a 10-day cooling off period." The outcome was that I had to wait 10 days to give myself permission to keep my number, and it therefore took nearly two weeks to get my broadband reconnected!

In that scenario, the person I spoke to knew what his job was, but he didn't consider the big picture either for me as the customer or for the business. There was a complete disconnect between the different parts of the business and, as the customer, it resulted in a far from ideal experience.

#2 Don't let perfect be the enemy of good

The point here is to understand where proxies are required and where good is enough to make progress. Speed is important, but you also need to be able to know when you've optimised something far enough. There will always come a point where you need to step back from one element and put your focus on another.

To return to our Formula 1 crew, it's about knowing when to stop working on the back tyres and instead focus on changing the aerofoil at the front of the car. These things all matter, but you have to consider what you might be neglecting in one area if your focus is consumed by another. One of the simplest ways to tell when you have optimised something enough is to step back and look at the whole picture. Ask yourself how much of a difference to the overall outcome will that tiny tweak actually make?

"I think brands need to continuously improve; a product or service will only ever not need to be improved when it is no longer sold. Technology is continuously improving and opening up new challenges and opportunities. The consumer's expectations, experiences, availability and need are always developing, so brands will always need to move with them.

"That being said, perfect is paralysis, so it's important that a brand understands they can improve but that does not mean they have not got something which is good enough for customers. It just means they need to continue to strive for it to be even better."

Aaron Bradley, VP of Technology & Innovation, Wella Company

You have to use benchmarks and proxies to recognise when optimising beyond a certain point will have a negligible effect on the outcome compared to the big picture. This is why it's so important for everyone to understand that big picture. If you're the person who's tasked with optimising the speed of the rear right tyre on a Formula 1 car, you will never stop trying to optimise that component if you don't have that visibility, and you won't necessarily recognise that your efforts could be spent much more effectively elsewhere.

In businesses, it's common to see this constant tweaking and revisiting of a product or service pre-launch. Nothing will be perfect when it's launched, so you have to stop striving for perfection and instead simply get it to a place where it is good and valuable. Think about the brand values we talked about in the last chapter. What do your customers value? Are they looking for convenience, exclusivity, or a specific price point? Does what you have created meet those values? If the answer is "Yes", do you believe that your product or service is good enough to launch?

Knowing what is good enough will be linked to your outcomes. When you are working on developing a minimum viable product (MVP) it is very easy to get caught up in deliverables rather than thinking about the outcome you are trying to achieve. To overcome this, a better way to think about it is as a minimum *valuable* product. This is a change in mindset, but one that will ensure that what you release provides value to your customers regardless of its level of complexity. You're starting with the end in mind by considering what value your product or service can provide, and working backwards from there to bring it to life, rather than creating a product or service and trying to advertise your way into consumers' lives.

The following diagram illustrates two different approaches to developing a vehicle to get you from point A to point B. How you develop that vehicle will depend on the outcomes and KPIs you set, and these will also dictate when you have reached "good enough." In the example, if you were only planning a journey of 10 minutes, a skateboard or scooter might be good enough. However, if you want to travel 100 miles, you will need a motorbike or car.

The point to take away from this is that whatever you're doing has to deliver progress. If it delivers progress, it's the right thing, but if it doesn't bring you substantially closer to your outcome, it's time to move on.

Less of this...

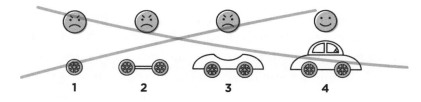

More of this...

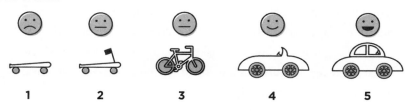

Figure 4.1

Az's take

Let's get ready to race

In my family, we love playing Mario Kart together. There are four of us and we often have race evenings. However, it's fair to say we probably spend more time deciding on our cars than we do actually racing one another.

Our son, in particular, will go through every single variable on the car to see which ones he wants, then he will go back and revisit his previous choices in case they no longer match up. The last time we had a Mario Kart evening as a family, we probably spent a good 20 to 30 minutes just waiting for him to go through this process, when it would almost certainly have been more effective if he'd made his

(continued)

(continued)

choices, put the car on the track, tested it, and then changed it once he'd seen how it performed. After all of that, he then lost.

In business, it can be easy to fall into this trap of endless iterations and tweaks, but it's really important to understand when you have made something good enough, and know that you can change it after it has launched if necessary. You test, learn, evolve, and so on; it's a never-ending cycle because you are never going to achieve perfection. To return to our Mario Kart evenings, we always had multiple races, so our son could have selected and optimised after each race. Then, by the end of the evening, he would have made progress towards the ideal kart and been ready to fight another day.

#3 Make sure you're planting trees

This principle centres on the need to balance short-term and long-term goals. There is a wonderful Greek proverb that states: "A nation grows great when old men plant trees in whose shade they won't sit." If you think about modern politics, most countries work on a four-year election cycle, and most politicians want to take short-term decisions that will have an impact during their tenure, but if they are only focusing on what's going to happen in the next three to four years, you've got ask who is looking out for the country over the long term?

Within business, the average tenure of a chief marketing officer (CMO) fell to just 40 months in 2020, the shortest it has been in over a decade.[1] At 100 of the mostadvertised US brands, the average

[1] Michaela Jefferson, "CMO tenure falls to lowest level in over a decade", *Marketing Week* (29 April 2021), available at: https://www.marketingweek.com/cmo-tenure-lowest-level/?cmpid=em~newsletter~breaking_news~n~n&utm_medium=em&utm_source=newsletter&utm_campaign=breaking_news&eid=20203150&sid=MW0001&adg=

tenure of a CMO was just 25.5 months. The problem with this is that CMOs, just like politicians, are going to make decisions that will deliver results during their tenure. As a result, they are making short-term decisions because that's what they are being measured on.

However, you have to ask the question: "Who is making the long-term decisions?" If you have a new CMO every 2.5 years, in 10 years that means your business will have had four different CMOs. Failing to make long-term decisions is one of the reasons why many businesses are struggling to catch up with their digital transformations because they have spent a decade making short-term, incremental decisions without considering the long-term decisions and bigger picture. As a result, many have fallen significantly behind.

"The perspective of success is heavily measured quarter by quarter, which drives a lot of urgency around ensuring that dollars invested are readily accountable to revenue and profit, with a pretty narrow lens."

Marisa Thalberg, EVP,
Chief Brand and Marketing Officer, Lowe's

Craig Smith (Co-Founder of Decidable Global Ltd) aptly refers to this as being similar to the "Premier League manager merry-go-round out." The point here is that someone needs to be taking that long-term view while also focusing on your short-term goals. Businesses need to take a leaf out of the book of the ancient Greeks and start planting some trees, otherwise they'll find themselves stuck out in the sun without a spot of shade in sight.

Rich's take

Small cuts lead to big consequences

Many years ago, a friend and I discussed setting up our own advertising agency that would be aimed specifically at the over-55s because well over half of the wealth in developed countries is in their hands, yet only a small proportion of advertising spend is aimed at them. Instead, the majority of the ad spend in most organisations focuses on emerging generations.

It's easy to see how the amount spent on advertising to the over-55s dropped over the years because each CMO who came in had made a small, short-term decision to take 2% of the advertising spend away from the over-55s and target it towards younger demographics.

However, after 15 years of everybody taking 2% from that category and redirecting it, you've lost a substantial portion of your advertising spend for the over-55s. Those small decisions added up over time and, because there was no consideration of the long-term goals, this left a gap that needed to be filled.

#4 Measure marginal gains *and* losses, or you'll be in hot water

If you put a frog in a pan of boiling water, it would jump straight out. However, if you put a frog in a pan of cold water and gradually increased the heat, one degree at a time, it would stay there and boil to death.[2] Why? Because it doesn't notice the small incremental

---

[2]No frogs were harmed in the making of this book

increases in temperature. In business, it can be very easy for marginal losses to slip by unnoticed; however, over time they can add up to big losses. This principle is about making sure you measure marginal losses and marginal gains so that you can prevent big losses from mounting up over time as well as accelerate marginal gains to make them add up to big gains.

In our experience, many businesses will overlook marginal gains or marginal losses and instead focus on things that have a big impact (or give the impression of a big impact, but we'll come onto that shortly). Even in businesses that are aware of marginal gains and losses, many fail to see their compound effect. It's also common for organisations to measure marginal gains, but to overlook marginal losses at a granular level. That might be fine if your marginal gains outweigh your marginal losses, but what if it's the other way around?

Former director of British Cycling David Brailsford is an excellent example of what you can achieve when you focus on making marginal gains. He broke down the various components that lead to success for cyclists, from their training and nutrition to the equipment they use, and focused on making marginal gains in each which, when brought together, resulted in many gold medals for the British cycling team.

Of course, marginal losses can compound in exactly the same way, but the outcome will be very different.

"Your efforts in marketing should drive outcomes, and your incremental efforts should drive incremental outcomes. Assessing each additional effort against a prior baseline helps make that case."

Doug Jensen, SVP – GTM & COE for Analytics & Activation,
Estée Lauder

The other element that is important to understand here is that statistical significance within data doesn't mean that it is significant for the business or that it is aiding progress towards your vision. Often in marketing, we will quote results that were statistically significant. You'll hear things like, "XYZ resulted in a 55% incremental lift between A and B." However, that incremental lift of 55% translates to £3 400, so it could be viewed as immaterial.

When you're using statistics, it's important to balance what is statistically significant with what delivers a material result. Sometimes, those results are not material at all; they are incremental. But where they're incremental you might see a small number turn into a big number over time if you automate and accumulate these marginal benefits.

Challenging this desire to share statistically significant results can be hard because in many organisational cultures there is an expectation of seeing this big difference in one hit, rather than incrementally and over time. There is certainly a balance to be struck here between demonstrating that you're not only making big changes, but also the right changes, and showcasing how your team is making a difference to the bottom line.

This is something we would encourage leaders to consider and communicate to their teams, otherwise you will keep getting reports with the big numbers in them, such as impressions, click-through rates, and marketing qualified leads, when what you actually want to see are figures relating to areas like the revenue you drive for the business and changes in brand perception. While the bigger figures might look impressive, they won't necessarily make a material difference to the business.

Equally crucial is being able to understand when a small number or result has the potential to be turned into a material gain. For example, if we walked into a meeting and told our stakeholders that we had two qualified leads, no one would pay any attention.

However, if we can say that we tested the system that brought us those two qualified leads in one particular sector in the northeast of England, and that we can automate and accelerate it across the whole of the UK in every sector, all of a sudden we could generate 22 000 leads, and that would be material. As soon as you realise that automation and scale can bring you a material number, you have to automate it as fast as you can.

Some businesses will carry out a test to prove their statistics, rather than taking an incremental result and evaluating how they can turn that marginal gain into a big number. Alongside this, it's important to always be thinking about the impact this can have on a business' revenue because, if we're honest, businesses don't care about leads; they care about revenue.

This is where marginal gains can be particularly important because they might look like a small thing when viewed in isolation, but when you extrapolate the revenue side of them you can measure them against the outcome you're trying to achieve and potentially show that these marginal gains can have a huge impact on what the business is trying to achieve.

The slimmest of margins

If you look at all the Formula 1 race teams, they track marginal gains and marginal losses obsessively. They break each race track into sectors and track their performance against their competitors sector by sector.

Each team will know that it is a tenth of a second faster in sector one than its main competitors, but the team will also know that it loses two-tenths of a second in sector two. If it is

(continued)

(continued)

losing two-tenths of a second in sector three as well, the team will know that after 66 laps, it will be way behind the leaders.

In Formula 1, it is never just about one race though. There are 22 races in a season so each team will know that if it doesn't fix these problems and make up for those marginal losses in one race, it will see the same losses in the next race. The team knows that the marginal gains or losses add up to winning or losing a given race, but it also has one eye on the bigger picture – the outcome of the whole season – and how those results will affect its standing in the championship.

Think back to the story Az shared about his family Mario Kart races. His son struggled to think beyond the race he was in, which meant he always looked for a big win rather than just focusing on making those small, incremental gains while reducing his marginal losses that would ultimately have seen him perform better over the course of an evening of racing. However, this also links to principle #3: Make sure you are planting trees. Not everyone on the team needs to be keeping an eye on the big, long-term picture, but it's essential that someone is so that she can direct and course correct as necessary.

There's no such thing as an average customer

There is one final point to bear in mind in relation to marginal losses and gains in that marginal figures might conceal a much bigger problem. For instance, we once worked with a client that had an average customer churn of 4%. On the face of it, that's a marginal number for this sector. However, closer inspection revealed that the client was losing 18% from its top group of customers and only 1% from its bottom group. That meant the company was bleeding its best customers, so all of a sudden that 4% churn figure ceases to be marginal.

The key here is context. Think back to the Healing Pyramid that we shared in Chapter 2 and how you need understanding to put the knowledge you have, which comes from data and information, into context. We see issues like the one we just highlighted happening on a smaller scale too. For example, many businesses look at bounce rate as a measure of the effectiveness of their website, but if a customer arrives on your website, reads an article, and then leaves, the intended activity is complete. Therefore, optimising against this metric will result in optimising for the sake of optimising. Furthermore, if you optimise for and measure bounce rate, you have to ask: "Are you any closer to understanding if you've sold more?"

The desire for "silver bullets" can be another area that trips up businesses. Often there is a perception that individual components of a solution drive a greater contribution than they actually do. A good example that challenges the risk of this is the story in the film *Moneyball* (based on the book of the same name), where baseball general manager at the Oakland A's Billy Beane and economics graduate Peter Brand come up with a model to create a competitive team by distributing certain attributes among their players across the whole team, rather than purchasing one or two "star" players.

Their approach had great success and, despite having a very limited budget, the Oakland A's won the 2002 American League West title and, at that time, broke the long-standing record for the number of games won in a row. Two years later, the Boston Red Sox used the same model to win the World Series. This was because the team looked at how it could best achieve its outcome and looked beyond the traditional game that focused on "star" players. Businesses often look for that one big idea, or a specific technology, that will catapult them to success. However, they could instead simply focus on doing all the smaller things well and still achieve great success.

In the world of Formula 1, it can be easy to assume that the driver is the most important part of the team, and securing a good driver for a season is the solution. However, there are so many other crucial components that make up a championship winning team, and even the best drivers in the world can't win if their pit stop is delayed or there is a technical fault with the car.

Just like in Formula 1, businesses need to empower their crew to do what is required, guided by an aligned purpose, if they want to deliver results consistently.

#5 Know what good looks like for you

Benchmarks are how you can tell what good looks like, which links back into principle #2. This principle is about how you use benchmarks to set priorities by consistently measuring them and using them to set targets. Benchmarks are especially important for larger organisations that are multi-brand and multi-market because a benchmark that works in the US won't be comparable to a benchmark that works in South America, which will probably be nothing like a benchmark in Vietnam.

The key to creating effective benchmarks is to have a framework that allows you to not only create your benchmarks, but also to turn those into consistent targets that can allow you to manage multiple brands and multiple models. You also need to ensure you are creating benchmarks for the right things within your business.

Imagine there are two friends walking in the jungle and they come across a lion. One of them stops, takes his backpack off and starts to put his trainers on. The other one turns to him and says, "Why are you bothering to put your trainers on, you're not going to outrun a lion!" to which his friend replies, "I'm not trying to outrun the lion, I'm trying to outrun you!"

What we're getting at is that you have to understand what's important to measure in terms of your business' performance, as we discussed in Chapter 2. In the preceding example, the first friend was benchmarking the wrong thing; he was measuring against the lion, whereas the second friend benchmarked against what was important to achieve their outcome – getting away! Your benchmarks don't have to come from inside your business either, you might set them by looking at your competitors or even by looking at organisations operating outside of your industry.

Let's return to Formula 1 to see how you can benchmark effectively against your competitors. Red Bull holds the record for the fastest pit stop at 1.8 seconds; Mercedes is second with a 2.1-second pit stop. Some of the other teams are around the 2.4-second mark. In this instance, the benchmarks are very clear. When teams are looking at how to improve and reduce their pit stop time, they might notice that they are changing the back wheels in 1.9 seconds, but that overall their pit stop is 2.1 seconds. They measure everything internally as well as against their competitors. Benchmarking can make the business better, as long as you focus on the right areas.

In ecommerce, for instance, there is often an obsessive focus on optimising and improving basket conversion. However, in many cases, those businesses are now getting towards the top end of their benchmark and pushing for a 1% or 2% improvement, but you have to question whether that effort would be better focused elsewhere because the gains have become so marginal. This is where looking at the big picture can really help because it might highlight that there are bigger opportunities for improvements elsewhere.

Compare outside your industry

When you are setting benchmarks for what good looks like, resist the temptation to only compare your business to others in the same sector. Often in commerce, businesses will look at other retailers in their space, instead of broadening that to compare themselves to the best buying experiences out there.

"As more and more people shop online, their expectations have changed. Convenience is still important, but people are looking for something more – a joyful experience of browsing and shopping online. The brands that win out will be those that engage their customers where they want to be met. Ecommerce is the new frontier for meaningful brand experiences."

Nicola Mendelsohn, CBE, VP GBG, Meta

That doesn't mean you have to aim for the best buying experience straight out of the gate, but you do have to consider customer expectations. For example, in online retail we all know that Amazon offers great buying experiences. As a retailer, you have to ask whether your service meets the business needs that are relevant in that context and whether it meets your customers' expectations. Does it need to be as good as Amazon? No, if you tick those first two needs and expectations boxes, it's good enough.

The key, whatever your benchmarks are, is to think of them in the context of the race you're trying to win, not only in terms of the area you're optimising, but also in terms of how that affects the business and your progress towards your big-picture vision.

Rich's take

Closest to the pin or best score on the hole?

Golf is a complicated game, but there are two golf competitions that illustrate the importance of context. The first of these is closest to the pin, which means whoever gets her ball closest to the pin wins. This can be compared to everyone else or just yourself. This type of competition is often used on charity golf days. Of course, in true competitive play, if you get closer to the pin it's easier to make the next shot, but being closer to the pin isn't how a winner is determined. The second competition is best score on the hole, which means the golfer with the best score on that hole wins. In this second scenario, the winning golfer might have his ball nowhere near the pin after his initial shot, but if he still makes his putt on or below par, he will beat a golfer who hits his ball closer to the pin initially but who goes over par to complete the hole. Essentially, the lowest score in the competition is the best score.

In Formula 1, team Williams and Haas are the lowest performing teams in recent years. They consistently finish bottom of the grid so it doesn't make much sense for them to benchmark themselves against the leaders. Instead, the focus is more on the teams in the middle of the pack, and making small, incremental steps to reach these before setting their sights on those at the top.

This illustrates that what a benchmark for good looks like is very much dependent on the objective and the outcome you're trying to drive. To have a valid benchmark, you have to be very clear on the objective you're trying to hit.

(continued)

(continued)

Az's take

There is also a capability angle to this in that Rich's handicap at golf used to be a six, whereas mine is probably closer to 60! So, Rich's objective might be to get closest to the pin, whereas my objective is usually to get the ball somewhere near the green.

We often see businesses setting up email marketing or CRM platforms and benchmarking themselves against organisations that have better quality tools and that have been at it for longer. They try to boil the ocean, when in actual fact they would be better off doing the simple things first and focusing on making progress.

#6 Make sure you don't just tick the boxes

We often hear businesses talking about how they want to "do" digital. They go away, do a digital project, and put a tick in their digital box. However, there is a big difference between being a digital business and "doing digital". It's not only digital where businesses do this, they also tick the culture box, the agile box, the transformation box, the AI box, and so on. However, they don't change their culture or become an agile business. They don't actually transform. The same applies to being customer-first. Businesses believe that they need to transform their customer experiences, but, despite talking the talk, very few are living it.

There is a fine line between doing these things to tick the box, and measuring the process so that you can see you're on the way towards real transformation, and turning motion into progress to deliver to the business.

Pizza or pasta?

In 2008, Pizza Hut announced that it was changing its name to Pasta Hut in an extensive rebrand costing millions. At the time, the restaurant chain was launching new pasta dishes on its menu and wanted to encourage customers to think differently about its restaurants and offerings.[3]

However, customers didn't respond well to the name change and, as a result, the chain reverted to its original name. It's important to consider the context in which Pizza Hut attempted to change its positioning. At this time, there was a trend for healthy eating and a number of other restaurant chains, most notably McDonald's, were attempting to reach that market by making changes to their offering and, in some cases, branding.

Pizza Hut was trying to tick that box of appearing more healthy despite making very few changes to its actual offering. At the time of writing, the biggest trends that businesses in all sectors are jumping on are diversity, equality, and inclusivity (DEI) as well as sustainability.

The key to embracing these trends effectively is to understand the context of why you are following that trend in your business, and to do so authentically. If you simply approach it from the perspective of ticking the boxes, the result will be a great deal of wasted motion and effort. Remember, ticking a box doesn't equate to progress.

---

[3] Charles Gemma, "Pizza Hut rebrands to Pasta Hut", *Campaign Live* (6 October 2008), available at: https://www.campaignlive.co.uk/article/pizza-hut-rebrands-pasta-hut/851119

#7 Make headless design a mindset

Headless design is a concept that was coined for commerce, but we believe organisations can apply and use this across every area of their business because, in essence, it is all about flexible design, or what we are calling *fluid transformation*. Gartner Research's "pace layering" strategy is a useful way of thinking about fluid transformation because it stems from the idea that not all parts of an organisation have to move at the same pace, and therefore agility can mean different things in different parts of an organisation.

Within its pace layering strategy, Gartner created three stages: Systems of Innovation, Systems of Differentiation, and Systems of Record. Systems of Record are the foundational systems, which you build once, you build right, and which Gartner suggests you only change every six to seven years. Systems of Differentiation are built with more flexibility in mind and you need to be prepared to change them every one to two years. Systems of Innovation are built to be highly experimental and flexible, and will change every few months.[4]

Each of these layers is essentially a stage within a business' transformation journey. The hardest part of any journey is getting off the ground. Think of launching a rocket, which requires a lot of momentum, energy, and effort to get it off the ground. To get to this point, you have to break down everything you're going to do into manageable chunks. Because of the effort involved to get your rocket off the ground, you also need to make sure that once it has launched it is going in the right direction, otherwise all that energy and effort you've expended will be wasted. In a business, this equates to wasted budget as well as time, and often means the project dies.

It's also important to understand that not all rockets are created equal because not everything you are trying to get off the ground will

---

[4]Gartner Research, Designing Your Pace-Layered Information Strategy (2016), available at: www.gartner.com

have the same complexity or persistence. You have to think differently about what you're getting off the ground and what stage you're at on your journey.

Do you need a boost?

When diesel cars were first released, they were ridiculously slow compared to petrol cars, so many manufacturers brought out turbocharged diesel engines to make diesel cars more competitive. However, even with these new engines, when you drove a diesel car there was still a lag before you reached a point of acceleration. The reason being that turbochargers were large and needed time to get going and build up momentum.

At the time, BMW took an innovative approach to this issue. It created a smaller turbocharger that could fire up much more quickly. This turbo would get to a certain stage and then quickly hand over to the larger turbo, resulting in less lag and an engine that was much closer to the performance of a petrol engine.

If you think of this in terms of our rocket analogy, it is as though BMW fired a small rocket to help the larger rocket take off, and then at the right point, the larger rocket takes over. It's a way of getting more speed more quickly, and building from one stage in the process to another to make your launch as effective as possible.

This is about building momentum incrementally because getting something off the ground is hard. You have to make sure that once you've got off the ground you lay the right foundations, achieve a certain point, bed it down, automate, accelerate, and use this work to build to your next stages.

Circling back to the mindset around headless design and agility, the point is that you have to think very carefully about what you're getting off the ground. Are you creating a System of Record or is this a System of Innovation that will change in a couple of months? The layer that your project falls into will determine how big the metaphorical rocket is and how much effort you put into it.

#8 Beware of initiative fatigue

Everybody on your crew needs to have a common purpose, and everybody has to be working in clear alignment with the outcomes you want to achieve. You have to track progress all the time as well as visualise and share the success. It's also essential to create short, quick milestones within long-term projects so that they are chunked up into short deliverables that have a clear link to progress so that all can see they're moving forwards.

What can happen, particularly if there are new people coming into the business, is that each new person starts a new project, and if each of those projects gains another three subsets you can see how quickly initiative fatigue could set in for the people (your crew) being tasked with delivering all of them.

The book *Switch*[5] by the Heath brothers shares an interesting piece of research conducted into the limits of perseverance and resolve.

In this experiment, a group of college students was invited to participate in a study about "food perception", and to report to the lab (and were asked to be a bit hungry when they arrived). They were

---

[5]Dan Heath and Chip Heath, *Switch: How to Change Things When Change Is Hard*, Random House Business (3 March 2011)

invited into a room that smelled amazing, and on a table in the centre of the room were two bowls: one with freshly baked chocolate chip cookies and the other radishes. Each selected because of their highly distinctive tastes.

Half the group (A) were asked to help themselves to the chocolate chip cookies, but no radishes. The other half (B) were asked to eat at least three radishes, but no cookies. Despite the temptation, all participants ate what they were asked to eat, and none of the radish-eaters snuck a cookie. That's willpower at work!

With the "taste study" officially over, another group of researchers entered with a second, supposedly unrelated story, to test group responses to problem solving. Each of the two groups were presented with a series of puzzles that were designed to be unsolvable, wanting to see how long each group would persist in a difficult, frustrating task before they gave up.

Group A, the cookie eaters who had not faced any temptation to resist the cookies in the taste study, spent 19 minutes on the task and made 34 well-intentioned attempts to solve the challenge.

Group B, the radish eaters, were less persistent. The group members gave up after only 8 minutes – less than half the time spent by the cookie eaters, and they only managed 19 solution attempts.

The point of this research was to show that your resolve has a limit, and the group that was told to eat radishes rather than biscuits exhausted much of its resolve in not eating the biscuits. To link this back to initiative fatigue, people only have a certain amount that they can give, and if you exhaust that on things that don't add value, there is a good chance their resolve and energy will run out when what they're doing is adding value. You have to make sure that you limit your initiatives and focus in the right areas.

You also have to continue to reinforce outcomes so that people can see the progress they're making and how their work is contributing to that bigger, overall outcome. This is where the principal needs to really engage with the crew. Otherwise, if the principal only focuses on what's going on in the environment, team members get fatigue as shown in our progress pyramid at the start of the book.

Az's take

Stand off

We got our first puppy, Alpha, in 2019 and he is a Pomsky (a Pomeranian crossed with a Husky), which is a breed that's renowned for being a bit stubborn and he has a very mischievous streak. Before we started going to training, and learning about positive reinforcement, we would tell him "No" when he did something wrong.

One day, I was in the living room watching TV when I noticed Alpha was chewing on something he shouldn't have been. I said, "No", and he looked at me as if to say, "F-off". In a firmer voice, I said, "Alpha, no". He continued to stare at me and just showed his teeth a little in the way that dogs do when they want to try and dominate a situation.

I kept making eye contact with him, which I'd been told was a sign that you're challenging the dog, because I wasn't going to back down. For about 20–30 seconds we were both just staring at each other. I wasn't backing down but neither was he. While still staring at me, Alpha stands up, walks over to the window, cocks his leg, pees on the curtain and then swaggers out of the room with a sense of pride. One–nil to Alpha.

The moral of that story is that you have to make sure that you're working towards the right outcome. I thought I was doing the right thing by challenging Alpha, but the outcome I got wasn't the one I wanted. In fact, I had never considered that being an outcome I *could* get. In business, you have to consider all possible outcomes and then work out the best course of action to achieve the outcome you want without wasted effort (like mine).

#9 Let success breed success

The key point here is that you need to be able to chunk opportunities down into small wins that you can track. These are your project waypoints, and they should all be focused around feeling good and getting everyone to celebrate. This builds enthusiasm and helps everyone who is part of your crew to keep up the momentum.

However, when you celebrate success, it is important to ensure it is material, and not just statistically significant, as we explained in principle #4. This is the counterbalance; it needs to be real success, a material outcome for the business and not just a percentage improvement.

For example, we recently ran a pilot project for an automotive client that led to 16 times more vehicle sales than anything else we'd been doing. That sounds great; however, that equated to 200 cars. This is a company that sells 80,000 cars a year, so while the result we got from our pilot project was statistically impressive, we would need to connect a lot of similar projects, with much greater value, for anybody to care. Going back to principle #4 earlier in this chapter, about measuring marginal gains and losses, if we could automate the process to repeat this activity, then it would be a more material result for the business.

Vince Lombardi, a former American football coach and NFL executive, said, "Confidence is contagious, but so is a lack of confidence." This speaks to the idea that the principal needs to keep the crew on track to achieve success initially and for that success to then continue. However, for this momentum to continue, the success you celebrate has to be material.

"Build cultures around failing fast, where failure is recognised as a positive realisation that the tested approach doesn't work. Adopt and implement these mindsets top-down to underpin bottom-up implementation. Support and encourage wins and losses."

Nicholas Cumisky, YouTube

As a business, you have to find a way of measuring each project and determining how quickly the investment you're making returns a meaningful benefit that you can track. One final thing worth noting when it comes to success breeds success is that making improvements at the top of your funnel will have a positive knock-on effect to what's happening at the bottom of your funnel.

Take the example we shared earlier about David Brailsford and British Cycling; the success of the British Cycling team led to more high-performing cyclists at the top of the sport as well as a greater number of people getting involved in the sport at the lower levels. This has not only improved the longevity of cycling as a sport in the UK, but has also led to higher performance among the people competing and getting involved at a grassroots level.

The outcome model

In turning motion into progress, we have discussed the importance of clear measures that track business outcomes, rather than the outputs required to deliver them. Of course, the outputs are essential, as we still need the required building blocks to deliver our outcomes.

The challenge, however, is that we often have many outputs that are not connected directly to the outcomes they are intended to drive. This happens for a bunch of reasons, many of which we have shared with you in this chapter and with the examples from *The Hitchhiker's Guide to the Galaxy* (namely, the story about the number 42).

There seems to be many projects that start with an idea of what a team wants to buy, without a clear understanding of the real question. Without this clarity of purpose, activities can become misaligned, and projects often end up overlooking the full range of capabilities and changes required that go way beyond the things they are buying.

Often, this can end up in pure motion that doesn't always translate to the required progress needed for success. A new cycle of buying then kicks off, in search of a more sophisticated solution, which we hope can advance our goal forwards. This is where an outcome model can really help.

An outcome model frames the question we are solving, clearly articulates the benefits of achieving that goal, defines the metrics we will need to track progress towards that goal (ideally from the KPI tree), and then breaks out all the business capabilities required to deliver on that ambition, in a phased and scalable way.

It starts with understanding the business problem, the value to the customer of fixing that problem, the business benefit achieved through fixing it, and lastly it considers the capabilities required to get there.

There is a sense of accomplishment in motion (buying things) because it feels like progress. We sometimes tell ourselves that to meet this goal, "We need some new technology (which may be the case), so let's buy the technology and we will have moved towards our goal." The reality is you haven't. All the capabilities that need to be in place for the technology to deliver its promise (how you work, a clear customer strategy, creative excellence, propositions that inspire consumers, automation, measurement alignment, repeatable processes, etc.) must harmonise, but the good news is that they don't have to all harmonise at the same time. You can define a big vision, but start small and, if you build the foundations with the right ambition, then successfully scale fast.

An outcome model frames how to develop this roadmap in a way that starts with the problem, ensures that all required factors to deliver that outcome are considered, and enables a prioritised approach to that roadmap so that returned value closely follows the investment plan.

It starts with: "What will make the car go faster?" not "Which individual department has the biggest budget and made the most compelling business case to buy something?" (Although they can, of course, be aligned.)

As is the case with the KPI tree, mapping this to develop multi-year roadmaps with clear measures and priorities is a complex and time-consuming process. So far we have given you a starting point for how to approach this, and when used alongside the KPI tree, these are two important catalysts for turning motion into progress.

We hope they give you some useful constructs; however, they are not intended to be substitutes for a fully fledged planning approach.

Progress accelerator

After you have identified what's important, prioritising your activities based on value will help you understand where to start. Use the outcome model exercise on our website to help with your prioritisation: www.motionintoprogress.com.

Highlights

We started this chapter by talking about how you have to make every shot count, but in order to do that you have to be able to learn, adapt, and evolve. As we've said already, there is no beginning, middle, and end for modern businesses; there is just a continuous beginning, a continuous season.

The nine principles we've shared in this chapter might not all be relevant to your organisation. Take the ones you find most useful and use them to make every shot you fire count. Your crew is there to build the momentum once the principal has communicated the vision and big picture, but to maintain that momentum there needs to be progress. This progress needs to be material and it has to be something that everyone on your crew can celebrate, which is why it's so important to set milestones and benchmarks along the way.

Formula 1 crews know that they'll never achieve perfection, but they also know that even if they're not on their A game they can still compete. They know what good looks like at every stage in the championship, whether that's winning the race or simply beating the team that's in front of them in the competition. While the crew has a laser-like focus on race day, there is always someone looking at the race in the context of the season. Marginal gains and losses can mean the difference between victory and defeat, which is why both are tracked so obsessively by Formula 1 teams, and it's no different in business.

Businesses can also learn from Formula 1 teams in terms of their approach to improvement. No component on a car gets changed without being meticulously designed and rigorously tested. In business, you have to embed the likes of digital, customer first, and agility into your organisation in order to see material gains. Anything else is just window dressing. This is about building the strong foundation you need to become agile, and be in a position to make the small and more substantial changes that improve your performance.

For all of this to work, both in a Formula 1 team and a business setting, everyone involved needs to be motivated and aligned. This links back to each and every person on your team understanding the purpose of what you are trying to achieve. Finally, success leads to confidence within teams and that elevates performance. Of the more than 100 constructors that have raced in the Formula 1 World Championship since it began in 1950, by the time we reached 2020, just nine teams had won more than one title. Ferrari tops this list (with 16 constructors' titles at the time of writing). As a business, you have to consider how you can take each win and build on that to deliver long-lasting performance.

Chapter 5
Row the Boat in Time
Creating empowered and aligned teams to achieve progress

"Alone we can do so little; together, we can do so much."

– Helen Keller

W e're jumping back to May 1997. The British Lions rugby squad has touched down in South Africa for its first rugby tour there since the end of apartheid. The media and pundits (both in the UK and South Africa) are viewing the three-match tour as largely symbolic. South Africa are the firm favourites to win, with the British Lions considered significant underdogs.

The first test is played at Newlands and, much to the surprise of the home crowd, the Lions win 25–16. The second test is set for Durban and, despite the upset of the first match, the home crowd is still expecting the Springboks to emerge victorious. There's a roar as the teams step onto the pitch and the match kicks off.

However, with the scores level at 15–15, the home crowd is getting quieter. It watches in disbelief as Jerry Guscot kicks a drop goal to nudge the Lions to an 18–15 lead. As the minutes tick down, and South Africa launches a furious attack on the Lions' try line, there's great anticipation in the stadium. However, the Lions team pulls together, closes ranks, and somehow manages to prevent any of the South African players from breaking through.

The 80-minute mark passes, the ball bounces into touch, and the Lions have, against all expectations, won the series. The final match of the tour allows South Africa to salvage some pride, but despite winning this third test comfortably, it's too little, too late for the hosts.

After the test, it was commented that, "The better players were beaten by the better team." When the team comes together, and you "row the boat in time", you can achieve more than you believed was possible. It is not what you have that really matters, but what you do with what you have.

Think about this in the context of rowing. If you have ever watched the Oxford/Cambridge Boat Race, or any competitive rowing event, you'll know that timing is everything. Every person on that boat has to row in time, for the entire duration of that race. If your efforts are coordinated, you have the best chance of winning the race, and to do that everyone on your team needs to be aligned. If not, you risk going in circles.

Az's take

Don't be shy …

Several years ago I was visiting Toronto with my family and we went to see a baseball game. Our son Leon told me before the game that he wanted to get on the big screen so I suggested that he and his cousin make a sign to hold up as this would increase his chance of being featured.

We were going to see the Toronto Blue Jays and one of its players was called Justin Smoak, so Leon made a sign saying, "We will, we will, Smoak you"! At the game, Leon was holding up his sign during every break when the cameras came up, and when he wasn't trying to get noticed by the cameras, he was shouting coaching directions to the players. I should add here that he knows nothing about baseball, but he was yelling "Hit it like you mean it!" and "Put your back into it!" which the crowd around us was finding really amusing.

At one point, he turned to me and disappointedly said, "Dad, I'm not getting on the screen and I really want to." I told him to keep holding up his sign because everyone else who was getting filmed had a sign. He persevered and eventually he appeared on the big screen. The only trouble was that he couldn't really see himself over the top of his sign!

Not long afterwards, the cameraman walked up the aisle near where we were sitting and the group of men in front of us, which had been enjoying Leon's banter, jumped up, grabbed him, and told him to film Leon. I grabbed my camera, getting ready to film Leon's big moment and suddenly I started to worry that he might get nervous with the camera on him. I was trying to work out what I should do if he became really shy.

As these thoughts were going through my mind, the camera turned on Leon and he jumped up on his seat, whipped his T-shirt off, and started swinging it around his head. Almost 20 000 people roared with laughter through the stadium. He was making the most of what he had available to him and, just like a leader has to with a team, I had to trust that he would handle the situation he was in.

Culture starts from the top ... but lives in the foundations

The first part of the book is based on the importance of strong leadership, and any culture of empowerment that enables people at every level to act with EQ and effectively manage that fluid process has to come from the top.

Leadership in business is like leadership in sport, where the aim is to ensure the right motivation, coherence, and ultimately performance from the team to be able to progress in the right direction. Think back to our Formula 1 principal. He sets the direction for the entire team and makes sure that each element is executed perfectly on race day.

In the same way in business, leadership is then cascaded into ways of working that define how a business collaborates to ensure that everyone is focused on the same goal. Strong leadership is needed to tie together all the elements we've discussed so far in the book.

As businesses and consumers evolve, we're continuing to see a change in leadership styles that are more diverse, inclusive, and future facing. This is something that our existing leaders need to consider in their approach to driving change within businesses today.

One of the things that is starting to change is the way that leaders influence the people within the business or, more importantly, the other way around. The people on the ground are increasingly helping to shape the direction of businesses based on their understanding of their own needs and desires.

We see collective insights being formed to drive business change and reduce the subjectivity of decisions. This is where the values, trajectory, and culture of your business is important. However, this has an impact as it creates subcultures with your business and, in some cases, even subvalues. This is fine and promotes autonomy and diversity of thought, but the critical factor for leaders is to ensure that the

overarching culture comes from the top and keeps everything connected. There has to be alignment.

Align the crew behind your purpose

Making sure you have alignment within each of your teams and
across your teams is the first main element we are exploring in
relation to rowing the boat in time. As we explained in Part One, the
purpose needs to be clear. Once you have a clear purpose, the next
step is to ensure everyone is aligned to that purpose.

To do this as a leader, you have to get everyone on board with
what you're doing and make all feel involved. There is a saying you
may have heard, "Culture eats strategy for breakfast". In a similar
way we believe that purpose eats passion. There is a lot of talk in
business about having passion and how this draws people into your
vision, but we believe that if you are clear on your purpose and
communicate that correctly, it will align people behind what you
want to achieve.

Former Merkle CEO David Williams says, "Managers get things
done through authority; Leaders get things done through influence."
Strong managers are generally excellent operators and are very task-
oriented. These people are a safe pair of hands and will get things
done. Leaders are great at creating a sense of belonging, driving
inclusivity, and aligning people towards a common goal.

Both of these roles set the culture within the business, but they
don't necessarily define the outcome. The definition is built on how
the people of the business execute that vision through your leadership
and that is then ultimately the perception of your brand to the outside world. Therefore, the ability to think beyond the current status
quo can be important when looking at your strategic vision.

A great example of a leader who set the culture within an organisation is Alex Ferguson during his time as manager at Manchester United. One of his core principles, and one of the things he credits for his success at the football club, was that he believed everyone at Old Trafford was part of the success of the team. It wasn't just about the players and the coaching staff, but about the people working in the shop, the cleaners, the grounds staff, and so on.

Ferguson also made a point of knowing the name of every individual that he came across in the football club because he felt so strongly that everybody was part of that culture and important for the club to come together. He knew everybody; when he walked into Old Trafford, he'd say "Hello" to all he met and ask them how they were because he wanted to instill that culture all the way through the organisation. In an interview, David Beckham revealed that Alex Ferguson once made him change his hairstyle (he had to shave off his mohawk) because it didn't meet the professional standards Ferguson set at the club and didn't fit with the perception he wanted people to have of the organisation as a brand.

Freedom in a box

The concept of freedom in a box encompasses several of the principles we shared in the previous chapter, in particular, knowing what good looks like for you and making sure that you don't let striving for perfection become the enemy of good. This approach needs to be ingrained in the behaviour and expectation of everyone in the business if it is to work effectively.

Jeff Bezos provides an example of how this can be done well. He is known for having coined the concept of 2P teams, which are teams that are no bigger than six or seven people and that can therefore be fed by two pizzas. He wanted to have multiple 2P teams within the business that had a very clear direction and purpose that were aligned to the overall organisation, but at the same time had autonomy and flexibility over how they approached the problem at hand.

This is freedom in a box. Under this model, there are multiple small teams, all solving individual problems and all aligned with a common purpose. This common purpose is the box that they operate within, but how they solve the problems themselves is much more flexible and determined by the members of each team. This is a big part of what has driven innovation at businesses like Google, Meta and Amazon.

As a leader, you have to find a way to strike the right balance between autonomy and alignment.

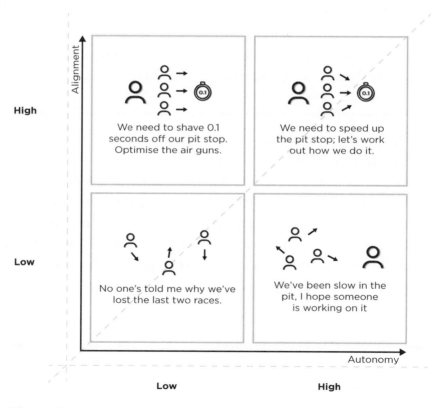

Figure 5.1

What you are aiming for is that top-right quadrant, where there is high alignment, the leaders are able to focus on which problems need solving, and then the teams are given the freedom to find the best solutions.

As Steve Jobs said, "It doesn't make sense to hire smart people and tell them what to do; we hire smart people so they can tell us what to do." While this principle is important, as the leader you still have to set the direction of travel. Autonomy equals empowerment, but it is understanding this direction, or the common purpose, that empowers people as well as giving them some ownership of that common purpose. When you can bring these elements together, people will feel a sense of belonging in the organisation and they will feel part of the transformation you're driving.

The key for leaders is to find the right measurements to track whether the autonomy and freedom within your teams is still aligning to the overall purpose of the organisation.

"If you want your teams to be engaged in their work, you have to make their work engaging. The most powerful way to do this is to give people the opportunity to experiment and solve problems that really matter. These problems won't be the same for every team or organisation. They may not even be easy to identify at first, but I am a big believer in challenging the status quo and encouraging bold, creative thinking to obtain your goal."

Paul Robson, President of Adobe International, Adobe

Is your organisation a spider or a starfish?

The analogy of the spider and the starfish is an old one, from the book *The Starfish and the Spider: The Unstoppable Power of Leaderless Organisations,* but a useful one for understanding the difference between a command-and-control hierarchical business and an autonomous organisation.

If you cut the head off a spider, the spider dies, and if you cut a leg off a spider then you have a seven-legged spider. However, if you cut a leg off a starfish, the starfish will grow another leg. Some starfish are even able to grow a new body on a severed leg (and then also new legs). In this example, the spider represents the command-and-control business, and the starfish represents the autonomous business.

In a command-and-control hierarchical structure, every decision runs from the tip of the leg, up to the head, and back down again. This makes it much more difficult to be highly responsive and adaptive in today's fast-moving world.

"Permission versus sponsorship is still such an important statement and it's something we've talked about a lot at Merkle. What it comes down to is that when a leader is a true sponsor of something, they hold themselves accountable to the outcome when they give permission either by funding something or simply allowing someone else to do something. The leader takes accountability for whatever the team or individual does, but they allow the team or individual the freedom to do it their way."

Craig Dempster, Global CEO, Merkle

What you are aiming for is to become an autonomous organisation with a clear purpose, and teams that function in a much more integrated and autonomous way. This will allow you to adapt and respond quickly to change, which is essential in the modern business environment. You want to be like the starfish and grow another leg.

The value of autonomy

In the modern world, the value of an organisation is increasingly tied into the experience it can build for its customers, so therefore being highly adaptive will have a positive impact on your business' value. Digitally native vertical businesses like Dollar Shave Club, Harry's, and Glossier are highly adaptive, highly integrated, have few silos, and view customers as the core of their business. This is what enables them to respond and adapt much more quickly than traditional organisations that might have more of a "spider" structure. They are small by comparison to their spider peers, but they have started to make a material dent in the competitive landscape.

The challenge, particularly for organisations that were built in the 1980s and 1990s, is that they were designed for total quality and not to make mistakes. To achieve this, everything had to be tied down and constructed with very strict rules and processes in place. They weren't built for adaptiveness, they were built to compete on quality. However, these organisations are now operating in a new era and are having to behave in a flexible, autonomous way even though they aren't designed to.

While this transformation to an adaptive "starfish" business from a hierarchical "spider" business won't happen overnight, you can already see the competitive advantage that starting that transformation has. Compare the value of Tesla to its automotive counterparts and you will see that Tesla is worth significantly more, in large part, because the company has demonstrated many of the characteristics of an adaptive organisation.

Becoming an autonomous organisation also has benefits internally, which can have a positive effect on a business' value. Empowering people and building an autonomous culture will naturally reduce attrition, which is a large problem in many industries and one that is only being compounded by significant skills shortages in many areas.

Are you just shuffling deckchairs?

Traditional organisations that are trying to transition to a more autonomous and agile way of working have to make sure they focus on genuine transformation rather than just ticking the boxes but changing very little beyond this.

There's one large organisation that latched onto the concept of agile and started an agile project in an attempt to move away from its more traditional structure. However, all this company did was take its people who were within the traditional command-and-control structure and reallocated them into squads and tribes without changing anything else. The company didn't change the measures of those squads or empower those people, it simply moved people from departments to squads, so nothing in the underlying business changed and, although the company feels it has ticked the agile box, it still isn't an adaptive organisation.

The best analogy we've found for this is like shuffling deckchairs on the deck of the *Titanic*. There's a lot of motion and it looks like the crew members are doing something, but they aren't achieving progress, and the changes they have made won't alter the fundamentals of their situation.

This concept of breaking down silos and encouraging collaboration is something we discuss in greater detail in Chapter 6. There will always be metaphorical walls in businesses, however what autonomy does is reduces the size of those walls and makes it easier for individuals and teams to work together across the organisation as a whole.

When sales and science don't align

When you are trying to introduce greater autonomy across your organisation, the key is to ensure that all of your teams are aligned to the vision set by the leader. However, when you have autonomy without alignment, there can be serious consequences for organisations and there are a number of cautionary tales that demonstrate the importance of getting that balance between autonomy and alignment right.

Theranos was a health technology company founded by Elizabeth Holmes in the early 2000s. She claimed to have invented a medical device that could do 200 blood tests off of a single drop of blood, and she raised $9 billion for this device.

All the scientists and engineers in the company were warning that this device wouldn't work and that it wasn't possible because you couldn't get that number of readings from a single drop of blood. However, the sales and marketing engine at the business was driving ahead. The market was hungry for a device like this and wanted it to work, so there was plenty of interest, which is how the company raised $9 billion.

The sales and marketing function was completely disconnected from the research and development function, to the point that the company eventually imploded and Elizabeth Holmes has been charged with wire fraud and conspiracy to commit wire fraud in the US.

This is a very extreme example of how a lack of alignment, coupled with autonomy, can damage (or in this case destroy) a business.

Selling the dream without the reality

Fyre Festival[1] is another example where a lack of alignment led to the complete failure of a business, not to mention being an example of very shaky ethics. Billy McFarland founded Fyre Festival, a luxury music festival, in 2017; however, there were fundamental flaws in the way the organisation operated from the beginning.

The festival started advertising and taking money for the event without having secured planning permission, organised accommodation, or signed up artists to take part. It was selling a dream but had none of the essential components in place to make it a reality. This lack of alignment between the dream and what was happening within the organisation meant it was never going to be successful.

What it should have done, with hindsight, was secure one of those main components first, before starting to take money. However, it chose to raise the capital first in the belief that it could use the money to get everything in place. What actually

(continued)

[1] *Fyre*, Chris Smith, Netflix (2019)

(continued)

happened was that it ran out of money and time, and the festival didn't even come close to delivering on its luxury promises.

The team members tasked with organising the event were in over their heads and, despite repeatedly being advised to postpone or cancel the festival, they pushed ahead anyway. Like the Theranos example, the enterprise led to McFarland being prosecuted for wire fraud.

Both of these examples also relate back to what we have already discussed in terms of measurement, and knowing when you have to change direction or do something differently. These are the decisions that need time as they can have an adverse effect on your business. In both the Theranos and Fyre Festival stories, the organisations didn't measure or disclose the measurement of the right things. They kept pushing ahead, despite the fundamental flaws underpinning both of their models.

With the Fyre Festival example, the organisation's biggest problem was that it had nothing in place and this didn't allow it to pivot. It didn't have the ability to change the nature of the event or to transform into a different type of business.

Contrast this with a product like Slack, which was initially developed as an internal tool for the company Tiny Speck during the development of its online game Glitch. In the context of the game, it didn't achieve expectations. However, the company saw an opportunity to repurpose Slack as a proprietary business communication platform and pivoted its use. In 2020 it was sold for $27 billion, not bad for a failed product!

When an organisation has teams that are aligned to a common purpose, as well as giving those teams and individuals autonomy, it is much more adaptive and therefore better able to pivot as and when challenges arise. Although traditional organisations may struggle to introduce this autonomy and alignment within their current structure, the examples we've shared here show that a lack of alignment isn't only a problem in existing organisations. It can just as easily occur in new organisations and cause serious issues if it isn't embedded within the business' culture from the start.

Who's on the bus and where are these people sitting?

In his book *Good to Great*,[2] Jim Collins talks about the importance of getting people on your bus, which refers to making sure that everyone within an organisation is aligned with the purpose and that those are the right people to have on your bus. Once you have the right people on the bus, you have to make sure that they are sitting in the right seat and playing the right role within the company. Finally, the bus will have to stop quite regularly to let people off. Despite your best efforts, you might not always hire the right people, so you have to find a way to let those who don't fit in with your teams or align with your purpose off the bus. In some cases, you might just have the right person in the wrong seat, or you might have to provide additional training to enable someone to contribute in the way you need them to.

What typically happens if you have people in the wrong seats, or the wrong people on your bus altogether, is that you end up with motion without any progress. A global telecommunications company that reorganised its structure in 2011 and, as part of that process, brought a lot of services and functions it had been outsourcing in-house.

---

[2]Jim Collins, *Good to Great: Why Some Companies Make the Leap and Others Don't*, Random House Business (4 October 2001)

During this reorganisation, the business moved its existing people into new roles, despite the fact that many of those people didn't have the skill set required to fulfil their new role. In creating these teams of people who didn't have the skills and experience to do their jobs effectively, progress stalled. On that particular "bus" several people were in the wrong seats and some of them probably shouldn't have been on the bus at all because they didn't fit into this new organisational structure. However, this isn't to say that you should always look externally. Sometimes the answer can be right in front of you, and promoting from within can be a very positive step if the opportunity is a good match to someone's skills. Essentially this comes down to balancing potential with experience. Getting people on the bus in the first place, and then ensuring they're in the right seats, is easy when your vision and culture is clearly defined. Take Disney theme parks as an example; everyone who works for them knows what kind of culture they're joining. Disney's focus is on instilling happiness throughout every one of its parks. Where possible, the company encourages its people to deliver magical moments to visitors. As a result, people go back time and again, despite the price being high, because they love that magical experience.

Az's take

Stepping into the Magic Kingdom

A few years ago, my family and I went to Disney for the first time, and although we'd heard all the stories, we didn't really know what to expect. Before the trip, my wife, daughter and I (being the geeks that we are) planned our whole two weeks on a spreadsheet, including scoring each ride. Our son was more interested in playing on his X-box while all of this was going on!

Whilst all of this pre-planning made the trip feel a little daunting, everything from our arrival at the airport to our first steps into our first Disney theme park felt magical. When we arrived, the woman at the reception explained everything we needed to know. The people operating the rides helped us understand how to make the most of each experience. The people serving our food always looked for ways to make things a little bit more pleasant. Throughout our time there, the kids would randomly get a nice surprise that meant the world to them, and when they smiled, we smiled.

Every person we encountered was on the Disney "bus" and each one of them was in the right seat. The result was an effortless and magical experience as a customer, in an environment where everyone seemed happy and genuinely excited to help. This is an aligned purpose executed with passion.

Making the most of what you have

As well as looking at the skills within your teams, you also have to consider the tools and technology that your people have available to them. We have often seen organisations throw all of their tools and technology out of the window because they deem this to be the problem, and replace them with something new.

However, it is often not the tools that are the problem, but how those tools are used. There is a wonderful video of a very unusual sport: brick racing. Each person is given three bricks and they have to cross a room always standing on those bricks. In this particular video, there are three participants. Two of them have a clumsy and slow way of stepping onto two of the bricks and moving the third one ahead of them, taking a step forward and repeating the process.

The third participant has developed a hunched walk with a rhythm that allows him to lift the brick that is under his lifted foot and move it ahead of him seamlessly. He makes the whole process look easy and like little more than a slightly odd stroll. All three of the men had the same tools, three bricks, but one of them used his bricks much more efficiently than the other two. If those bricks represented technologies in most businesses, the first two would have thrown out their bricks and bought new ones.

Rich's take

Make do and win ...

I once went to a golf day at my local club and, as part of the event, a professional golfer attended and participated in a competition with those of us who were attending. The competition was to hit the longest drive on the fairway.

We all took our shots with our drivers; not all of them went straight, indeed some of them didn't get very far at all. Then the professional golfer stepped up to the tee and instead of using a driver, he had a range of different "clubs". The one that impressed me most was a piece of hose pipe with the head of a three-iron tied to the bottom. His party trick was to hit his drive using the hose pipe with the three-iron, and he knocked it straight down the middle of the fairway, farther than any of us.

He also had putters and the back end of an umbrella, and whatever he used to hit the golf ball, he would smack it straight down the middle of the fairway. It certainly wasn't about the quality of his clubs, it was all about what he could do with what he had.

The majority of people, even if they were solid golfers, wouldn't be able to use that "tool" in the same way that he did. He had perfected how to hit a ball, and what he hit it with didn't matter that much.

Raising and training unicorns

We know unicorns don't exist, but the word is often used today to describe multi-skilled talent in organisations.[3] Hootsuite Chairman and Co-Founder Ryan Holmes describes unicorns as "a member of the staff who possesses a unique set of qualities that make them extremely rare and valuable."

In modern organisations, it's becoming increasingly important to raise and train unicorns because they offer enormous benefits in the workplace, and their qualities make them extremely rare and hard to find.

Az's take

Left or right?

I'm right-handed and I always trained right-handed when I was playing tennis. However, as soon as I reached county level as a junior, coaches made me regularly train left-handed because they wanted me to develop my skills and coordination with my left as well as my right hand. This was part of the

(continued)

---

[3] Sodexo, *8 Qualities of a Unicorn Employee* (2019), available at: sodexo.ph/blogs

(continued)

coaching system and the idea behind it was to make both your sides equal, to avoid you having a weaker side that could let down your game. It was about evolving my foundation rather than reengineering my playing style, much like in boxing where boxers who have an orthodox stance are often also taught to box southpaw as a differentiation in their skills.

This was certainly challenging at times, but it made me a better all-round player. A large part of this was due to the improvements in my serve. The serve is the only shot in tennis where you have full control over what happens and the left hand is a huge component in your serve as a right-handed player.

What the coaches were doing was training two-handed players in a one-handed context. In addition, the new and additional skills we picked up through this training enriched what we already had in our tool box.

While not everyone in your business needs to be able to do everything, there is a great deal of value in raising unicorns. Having people in senior positions, in particular, who can work cross-functionally can make a significant difference to your operations and allow you to lower the walls between various business silos as well as reduce the risk of holding knowledge within pockets of your organisation.

The concept of training your weaknesses or training in areas that aren't necessarily essential is one that is often overlooked in business. Unicorns are the people whom everyone wants working for their organisation. We've already said that experience is the next battleground in business. Every organisation and brand is looking at how to evolve its experience, but it's the unicorns who build those experiences and fight that battle. As a result, there's a lot of competition for those "right" people.

If we go back to Formula 1, a great example of a unicorn here would be Lewis Hamilton, seven-time world champion. Not only is he a phenomenal driver on the track, but is often one of the last people off the track after the race as he works with the team of engineers and analysts to find new ways to help the team improve the performance of the car. He is also passionate about supporting causes that prevent social injustice off the race track to ensure that his role influences more than just the racing community.

If you have unicorns in your organisation, you want to keep hold of them. You also want to get everyone involved in delivering the best experience possible for your customers. As Richard Branson said, "If you look after your staff, they'll look after your customers. It's that simple."

As well as finding the right people for the right seats, you also have to consider the diversity of skills across your teams and the diversity of the people you employ to ensure they reflect your customers and enable you to look at different perspectives across your business.

This whole concept of rowing the boat in time is about having the right team in place, which doesn't necessarily mean they all have to be the very best. Herb Brooks was the US ice hockey team coach in 1980. Following the trials for the team, he picked his squad and gave the list to his assistant coach Craig Patrick, who looked at it and said, "You're missing some of the best players." Brooks' response was, "I'm not looking for the best players, I'm looking for the right ones."

To put this in context, at this time, Russia was the dominant national team and it was unstoppable. The Russians had great talent, but the difference between the Russian national team and its competition was that it put that talent into a system that worked for the benefit of the team.

By the time Herb Brooks was picking his squad in 1980, the Russian team had proved time and again that it could beat the best players the NHL had to offer. Brooks took a group of younger players, who had the mindset of wanting to work as a team as well as diverse skills on the ice, and he brought them together. This US team went on to win the Olympic gold medal at the 1980 games, beating Russia who was the four-time defending champions in the semi-finals, and going on to defeat Finland in the gold medal match.

This focus on diversity of skills and talent, and on finding the right people for the team, is something all businesses can learn from. It's just as important to consider diversity in your teams in terms of how those teams represent your customers.

Establishing a programme that helps to drive the preceding values is important, but it's even more critical to ensure that these are ingrained into your day-to-day operations as a business. Authenticity is an important factor as it's easy to see when this agenda is important to businesses or when it's bolted on. Don't tick the box; as leaders, it's our responsibility to ensure that we are continuing to be forward-thinking in our approach to workforce representation and culture. This, in turn, will see your business scale and diversify in skills and attributes that could help to positively transform the business from the inside out.

Efficiency: The final piece of the puzzle

When it comes to the concept of row the boat in time, you have to think about how you can be efficient with how you're using your resources, how you're using your people, and also how you're building your culture. It's important to consider where you can productionise and create processes and frameworks around what you do that will make your business more efficient, without losing autonomy.

A field that has great inefficiency is data science. In many businesses, data scientists can spend as much as 90% of their time collecting, cleaning and organising data and just 10% of their time analysing the data, despite the fact that their value comes from the analysis. That means 90% of their time is essentially wasted effort. Inefficiency will cripple any of your efforts to create alignment and build autonomous teams that are made up of the right people with the right skills for the job.

Your resources, platforms, and infrastructure need to be efficient, connected, and accessible so that your autonomous teams can deliver the results you're striving for. What can happen when you don't have efficient systems in place? Take a business that went through a tender process for a new omni-channel capability that then took two years to add tags to its website. This was due to the organisation's siloed structure where legal and marketing were not measured on the same objective.

If you don't row the boat in time, your boat just ends up going round in circles. When this happens, many organisations make the mistake of throwing money at the issues they perceive and then wonder why they are just going round in circles. So many of the organisations that we've worked with have invested in pretty much every product and tool you need from a marketing perspective, but many of these companies don't have the skills within their teams to implement them. They can't turn motion into progress.

A modern example of this is Elon Musk's first principle thinking. If he hadn't focused on improving the efficiency of the batteries used in electric cars, for example, the adoption of electric vehicles would have been slower.

We've mentioned Amazon and its AWS service earlier in the book, but it's interesting to note that Amazon developed this technology initially because it needed a way for its data scientists to access their data via the Cloud if it wanted to use data to drive the business. Of course, Amazon has since sold it to other organisations and it's now one of the largest parts of Amazon's business, which is just incredible.

Amazon is also one of the first and most effective examples of headless commerce, which we mentioned in Chapter 4, but one of the reasons it has been able to do this is because of its flexibility and the way it has become adaptive around its technology capabilities.

Why aren't we moving faster?

One final point on efficiency is that cost cutting doesn't necessarily equate to efficiency. There are many examples of organisations that make cuts to their teams to deliver cost efficiencies and then wonder why they aren't moving faster. The answers are usually because they have made the cuts in the wrong places or they have failed to consider the outcomes that they're trying to achieve and the impact of those outcomes on the business' progress.

We talked about the concept of freedom in a box, and that box needs to be a lot bigger in some organisations than it currently is; otherwise, you won't see the benefits of that autonomy in the context of the whole organisation. Businesses have to be bold and be prepared to potentially let their people make some mistakes along the way; otherwise, they will find they are constantly hitting roadblocks in their quest for progress and people will simply find ways around the guard rails that they put in place.

The key is to find the right balance between autonomy and efficiency; otherwise, you have process for the sake of process, which only holds you back. You can use measurement as the control, to provide you with a tangible way of seeing whether the outcome you want has been achieved. This is also why knowing the outcomes you're aiming for is so important. During cost-cutting exercises, many businesses focus on headcount. However, whilst headcount may meet cost reduction needs, it often significantly impedes progress because it doesn't always equate to value.

"The organisations that excel and are most successful will be the ones that have a culture that can keep up with the pace of change, through their own change, because we're talking about a world that's constantly evolving so you have got to be agile. The organisations that can scale and still be agile are the ones that will emerge as the winners and those that are not agile and that don't have the culture for agility and speed of change will struggle."

Craig Dempster, Global CEO, Merkle

Highlights

We have covered four key principles in this chapter: alignment, autonomy, skills and talent, and efficiency. You need alignment to drive autonomy; for autonomy to work you need to have the right people with the right skills to do the work; and you also need an efficient platform to enable those people to do the work in a way that doesn't hold back your business.

In a similar theme to "culture eats strategy for breakfast", the Heath brothers said that, "If culture eats strategy for breakfast then purpose trumps passion." The idea being that if you have a clear and aligned purpose, then culture and strategy will follow.

Everything to do with the culture in your business needs to be driven towards that purpose, including the likes of your social impact and responsibility, which makes a huge difference. This purpose has to be ingrained in everything that you do, and you also need to measure it from a cultural perspective. We always talk about moving forwards and looking forwards, but every so often you need to look backwards to see how far you've come.

Rich's take

Paddling out

I grew up in South Africa and spent a lot of time surfing and paddle skiing. When you're paddling out in South Africa you're confronted by very big waves, sometimes 3m or higher. You always have to go under the wave and, as you surface, there's always another wave looming over you. The only way to measure your progress is to look at how far you've come from the shore because if you look ahead, all you'll see is another wave.

Within business it can be harder to measure some of these softer elements so you have to think about what the proxies are for the behaviours you're trying to create and make sure you're looking at the right things without getting too bogged down in data.

This is particularly important where autonomy is concerned and you can use flow efficiency to track the effect autonomy has on the whole business rather than simply measuring autonomy in an individual environment. You need to have measures to show that autonomy is working beyond a single department because that department can't do anything in the context of the wider business if the organisation around it is inefficient.

Let's come back to our Formula 1 team and look at the pit crew as an example. There are typically around 20 people involved in a single pit stop. Each one is exceptionally well trained and each one knows exactly what the individual job involves. However, that knowledge is underpinned by the understanding of what it means in the context of both the race and the overall season.

A pit crew might be delivering the fastest pit stops on the grid, but if the car isn't performing, the driver isn't on form and the processes to develop and improve both the technology and performance isn't in place, then ultimately that fast pit stop won't make a difference to the eventual outcome, either in an individual race or across the course of a season. The principal has to lead from the front to set the purpose and direction of travel with clear measures, and once that is in place, it's crucial to build and align teams around this purpose.

Part Three
The Season

The unmistakable sound of 40 Formula 1 engines gunning as the light turns to green on the starting grid gets the crowd fired up. Its cheers and shouts are drowned out by the distinctive roar of the cars whizzing past. The race is underway!

The sun bakes the tarmac of the track and, after the usual jostling for position, the drivers spread out a little with the leaders breaking away from the rest. On lap 22, one of the cars in the middle of the pack suffers a burst tyre. The driver loses control on turn three, spinning into the barriers and clipping the wing of another car on its way.

The nose of the car crumples as it hits the barrier, and debris and dust flies into the air. The driver hits their steering wheel in frustration, climbing out of the vehicle as the safety marshalls rush towards them.

The drivers immediately behind dodge the debris that scatters the track and it isn't long before yellow flags are waving at the side of the track, slowing the race to allow all the drivers to safely navigate this section of track until the debris is cleared.

As soon as the crash happens, the principals of every team spring into action, shouting directions to their respective crew and briefing their driver over the radio, doing everything they can to maintain their advantage or gain on their competitors during the disruption. They all know that these incidents that are outside of their control can affect

*their performance across the season. Valuable championship points
can be gained and lost and, for some, even an end to their hopes for
a season.*

*The principal whose car has crashed is focusing all their energy on their
remaining driver, but they can't hide their frustration. They know
there will be other seasons, but failing to finish in this race will put
their driver too far behind the leaders to have any hope of a top-three
finish in either the drivers' or the constructors' championships this year.*

A standard Formula 1 season includes 22 races at tracks around
the world. Each qualifying session and race day will be different.
Aside from the tracks themselves being different, each team will
have to contend with whatever weather conditions occur on the day.
Incidents, like collisions, can change the shape of a race. While the
principals and their crews can prepare for a given track, they cannot
control what weather they have on the day or what might happen in
the course of a race.

They have to adapt quickly, change their strategies, and read the
external environment to give their driver the best chance of succeeding on the track.

In business it is no different. What we have discussed in Parts
One and Two are the elements of your organisation that you can
control. However, in Part Three we are looking at the enterprise
environment. This is the environment you operate in, where you have
to account for competitors, economic conditions, and many other
factors that will affect your business.

These aren't fixed conditions, they are constantly changing, which
is why it's so important that you are able to adapt to meet them. As
we said in the first chapter, you adapt or you die. In these final three
chapters, we are going to explore how your organisation can make the
best of conditions that are outside your control.

In Chapter 6, we are going to focus on what is happening to your organisation and how the concepts and principles we've described can be brought together across your business as a whole. Chapter 7 is about the business environment and how you can respond and make the most of all of your opportunities. In Chapter 8, we explore the concept of "going for the albatross" and how you can tell when you should go for those big, bold ideas and when you should hold back.

Chapter 6
Turn Headwinds into Tailwinds
Positioning your team to adapt to the external environment

"When a management with a reputation for brilliance tackles a business with a reputation for poor fundamental economics, it is the reputation of the business that remains intact."

– Warren Buffett

We're jumping back to 2011 and a very rainy Montreal in Canada. It's the day of the Canadian Grand Prix and, after 40 of the 70 laps, Jenson Button is in last place. By this stage of the race, the safety car has been on the track three times and there has been a two-hour suspension due to the rain.

Button has collided with McLaren teammate Lewis Hamilton and, on lap 37, with Ferrari's Fernando Alonso. At the restart after the third outing for the safety car on lap 40, Button is in an unenviable position at the back of the pack. However, his team made one crucial decision earlier in the race: he was the first leading driver to switch from wet to intermediate tyres.

As the conditions improve, and Button is moving up the pack as other drivers pit, his team again takes a bold decision to switch from intermediate to dry-weather slick tyres. Button still has a lot to do as he enters the final six laps of the race, despite having made it back to the leading group. He's in fourth, with Schumacher, Webber, and Vettel still ahead of him.

On lap 65, Button overtakes both Schumacher and Webber to jump to second place, with Vettel now in his sights. As the cars zoom around the track on the next four laps, Button increases the pressure on race leader Vettel. On the final lap, Vettel allows his wheel to drift just wide of the dry line, sending his car into a half-spin. Button doesn't need a second chance and takes the lead, flying across the finish line to see the chequered flag fall and claiming a remarkable win.

Jenson Button came from last place to win that race, but he didn't have to overtake 20 cars on the open track to do that. His team took the correct strategic decisions that allowed him to leapfrog many of the other drivers when they were forced to pit to change their tyres.

As much as this is about making sure that you take the opportunities that are presented to you, it's also important to ensure your organisation is in a position to maximise those opportunities, which comes back to what we have discussed in Parts One and Two of this book: setting a clear vision and driving alignment around that vision across every level of your enterprise. Another element to consider is how your enterprise is organised internally because, as we have already explained, a disconnect between departments often creates friction. While far from ideal, these are headwinds that you have control over.

How high are your walls?

In his book *Rethinking the Corporation: The Architecture of Change*,[1] Robert Tomasko uses the analogy of trying to throw a tennis ball over a wall when it comes to navigating across the multiple silos that exist in many organisations. Each department has a wall, and the more senior the people you're trying to reach, the higher the wall that surrounds them. That means you'll need more attempts to get the ball over that wall.

His point is that it's tiring to throw the ball over those walls, and the more walls you have to throw your ball over to reach the other side, the more tiring it is. In building these metaphorical walls between your departments, you're creating headwinds within your organisation that both your teams and your customers have to navigate.

"Obvious barriers to delivering the pace of change required to meet customer needs include brands having siloed ways of working that drive friction into a seamless customer experience. Corporations that drive to reduce those silos find common incentives and high-performing cross-functional teams. Making everyone accountable to consumer goals is definitely an unlock."

Doug Jensen, SVP – GTM & COE for Analytics & Activation,
Estée Lauder

The more adaptive your organisation is, the fewer the walls between your departments and the easier it is to collaborate. Developing autonomy within your teams, as is discussed in

---

[1] Robert Tomasko, *Rethinking the Corporation: The Architecture of Change*, Amacom (7 January 1993)

Chapter 5, is important for reducing those walls, but in order to have autonomy that drives progress, you need to start with alignment to a common goal, which may be closer than you think.

Flicking the switch

There is a principle within kinetic particle theory called Brownian motion, which refers to the way in which particles move in all different directions and in a random pattern when they are suspended in water or gas. There is a type of smart glass that includes a thin layer of liquid between the panes of glass based on this principle.

These suspended particles are organised randomly and, if you shine a light on them, the way in which they are spread out prevents that light from getting through, making the glass appear opaque. However, if you flick a switch and apply voltage to the glass, the particles align and the glass becomes transparent, allowing you to see through it.

When all the particles are moving in random directions, it looks like chaos, but in actual fact it often doesn't take that much to align them and deliver clarity. In our experience, many organisations are not that far away from their switch; they are simply struggling to find it.

Creating this alignment is what allows you to turn a headwind into a tailwind. Instead of having to fight your way forwards, you begin to drive forwards easily and build up positive momentum.

Lowering the walls

Businesses are designed to mitigate risks and that often means they lock things down, whether that's in terms of spending through the finance department or restrictions imposed by legal and so on. These restrictions, whether they're legal contracts or spending limits, are all in place for good reasons; however, they can create these high walls in businesses and that, in turn, create friction.

In the context of each of those individual departments, what each is doing makes sense; however, when viewed in the context of the overall business, it becomes a headwind. You're putting up bigger walls and that makes it harder to throw your balls over them. This is where the concepts of alignment and autonomy become so important.

Rather than seeing these parts of the business as nonfoundational in terms of what you do as a brand, the key is to make them more ingrained as part of the process. The best way to do this is take them out of their silos and embed them into multidisciplinary teams where their measures drive connected behaviours.

Blending organisational silos

A great example where this has been done well is in Aviva. The company has taken people from the relevant business functions, including departments like finance and legal, and embedded them into their agile teams. This has had a number of positive effects on the operations of the organisation. Those individuals are better aligned with the organisation's purpose; they're committed to achieving the overall goals, but they are also part of the entire process instead of being one, hidden subset within it.

This strategy created incredible accountability as well because within those teams everyone was aligned to the same outcome, and the result was that Aviva became much more productive in the way that it was delivering its customer initiatives.

Reducing the headwinds within your business, like Aviva has done, will not only make you more productive, but it will also allow you to capitalise on opportunities you might otherwise have missed out on. Being able to recognise when you not only have these metaphorical walls, but when they are too high, is part of the challenge, but one that can be solved when you step back and look at the big picture.

When the wall is too high

As we've said, some organisations put up walls and, in doing so, miss incredible opportunities. Back in 2014, a large financial services company came to us looking for a solution to a particular issue it was having. We built a solution, demonstrated that it worked, and presented it to five of the company's managing directors.

They were incredibly excited about what we showed them; all of them were amazed that we had built a solution that had been talked about for so long but that hadn't been achieved. The managing directors were chatting amongst themselves about where they might roll it out first, when the person in charge of the company's technology raised his hand and said, "Can I just check, what is the technology you're using for this?"

We explained that it wasn't one piece of technology, but that we had stitched three pieces of technology seamlessly together. His response was, "Well that changes everything. We don't want three pieces of technology." We asked, "Have you seen anything in the market that is one piece of technology that can solve your problem?" The answer was "No."

Then we asked, "Will what we've presented to you solve your problem?" The answer was "Yes."

However, the managing directors were adamant they didn't want our solution because it was three pieces of technology instead of one. They left and never came back. They spent five years buying multiple tools, none of which have ever done the task, simply because they had put up walls that separated IT, data, and marketing. The lost opportunity cost from this siloed approach is enormous.

Finding the balance

In his 1997 novel *Dark Nature*, Lyall Watson explores "the invisible order that preserves the delicate balance between civilised society and anarchy." He suggests that all of us have a dark side and this is only kept at bay by the thought of consequence.

If you're a parent, you have probably wrestled with the relationship between actions and consequence.

On a broader societal level, you can see this concept at work in that the majority of people are law-abiding citizens because they fear the consequences of breaking the law. However, when you think about the number of people in the UK compared to the number of police, you can quickly see that law enforcement wouldn't be able to maintain order if everyone rose up against the law.

We're not suggesting that fear of consequence should exist in business, but proper governance still requires a healthy regard for measures and alignment. In a business context, this is all about finding the balance between departments and organisational functions. A classic example that we frequently come across is global versus local.

A global organisation has to balance this desire for consistency with the need for flexibility within local markets to allow for different cultures, languages, and so on.

There is a similar balance to be struck between flexibility and repeatability. To make something repeatable in business, organisations will often create a framework that should be repeated across all markets, but in doing so there is zero flexibility. The key is in finding the right balance between the two.

Within the business itself, there are decisions around how to set up teams – such as whether you want a federated model with lots of small teams or a centralised model with one large team – that you also have to balance. All of these elements become important decision points for businesses on their way to becoming adaptive organisations.

To make the right decisions in these areas, you need clear principles to be ingrained in the business moving forwards because if you don't strike the right balance, you will lean too far one way or the other, neither of which will help you to make progress in the long run.

Finding the right balance across your organisation stems from all people across the entire business understanding what they are doing in the context of working to achieve the business' goals. The final piece of the puzzle is the season you find yourself in. When you have these other elements in place, it is much easier for everyone in your organisation to adapt to changing external circumstances.

The blinking business

The discipline of physical cosmology has a theory called the "Big Bounce", which proposes that the universe will at some stage rapidly collapse to the state where it began and then initiate another Big Bang, and so in this way the universe would last forever, but would pass through phases of expansion (Big Bang) and contraction (Big Crunch).

The theory has been described as if the universe is going "blink-blink" with every big bang and big crunch: the blinking universe.

In the world of business, many organisations have their own version of "blink-blink." They go from being centralised to decentralised and back again, always struggling to make either end of the scale work. They give autonomy and then take it away, outsource and then insource. The reality for the majority of these enterprises is that the optimum is somewhere in between. There is no clear measure for where on this scale a business should set because this will very much depend on the business in question.

However, when your organisation has its North Star, you can set clear measures against the blink-blink to help you find that optimum point between efficiency and effectiveness, local market and global market, centralised and decentralised, in-housing and outsourcing, and so on. This is a continuous balancing act, and having that North Star will help you find the middle ground that works for your organisation.

Understanding that business isn't a Boolean option, where it is either this or that, but a fluid, sliding scale can really help you find that balance. Where on the scale your organisation sits will depend on what the need is and what you are trying to achieve. This also ties in with what we talked about in Part One in relation to businesses in the modern world requiring multiple strategies to survive.

This is about more than simply having options; it's about a constant process of testing, learning, evolving, and course correcting to chart the best course for the future. You might start with five strategies, but discover three of them have undesirable outcomes, and therefore you only move forwards with two. The key is to never stop that process of testing, learning, and evolving, and having the flexibility to adjust your structure and models accordingly to have a headless transformation mindset.

> ### *Rich's take*
>
> #### Seeing shades of grey
>
> I studied a BSc in Hydrogeology, which included zoology and botany at university, and I really embraced the idea of Darwinian evolution. I remember ending up in some very interesting debates with some of my friends who were largely in two opposing camps: spontaneous generation versus divine creation.
>
> Although they would discuss very passionately from their respective perspectives, there was an agnostic group that was content with the reality being somewhere between the two ends of that spectrum. This group suggested that if you read the book of Genesis in the Bible and compare it to the history of evolution, there is a strong correlation between the two, except that, of course, the history of evolution spans a few billion years rather than just seven days.
>
> The point to take from this example is that there are often multiple shades of grey, with no obvious right or wrong and, in that situation, you have to manage those and find the one that best suits your needs at any given time.

Because there is a great deal of grey in the modern business environment, businesses need to make decisions after assessing what's available to them and what they are trying to achieve rather than by planting their flag firmly in one camp and only seeing what's happening from that perspective.

There is a story that before employing any senior member of staff, Henry Ford would go for lunch and, if the candidate put salt on the food without tasting it first, he wouldn't employ them. The reason being that this person would be prone to making decisions without all the facts.

Before the era of LinkedIn, one government organisation was receiving so many job applications at one point (this was obviously before the days of emails) that they would separate them by colour, and every application that arrived in a brown envelope instead of a white envelope would just be binned without even being opened. The logic for the recruiters at that time (and we're talking many years ago because this clearly wouldn't fly in an inclusive workplace today) was that the white envelopes were better quality, so they used this as one of their qualification criteria to reduce the number of applications they looked at.

Of course, the flip side to this is that if you have to have all the facts before you make a decision, you may procrastinate and never take any risks at all. As with the other examples we've shared so far, the best option lies somewhere in between, in that grey area. When you find your best option, you can use it to create the right kind of environment at your organisation.

Creating an environment where your business can flourish

While there will always be circumstances and situations that are beyond your control as a business, you can take certain steps to create an environment within your organisation to allow it to flourish. The concept is best explained with the following diagram.

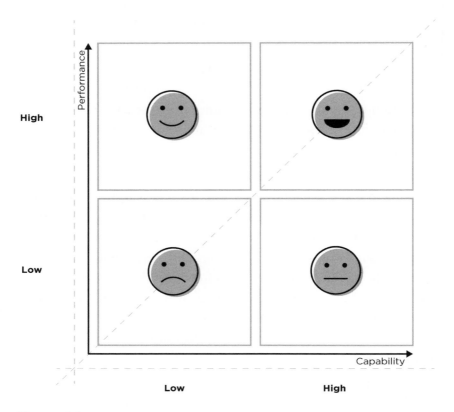

Figure 6.1

The diagram shows that you have to balance the things that you have with what you do with them. A big part of that is creating an environment where your tools and capabilities can flourish, and where your teams have the right level of autonomy to do the same, as is discussed in Chapter 5.

The top right in that grid is where you want to be, where you have all the tools you need, and you're doing a lot with them. However, it is preferable to have fewer tools, but better to be doing a lot with what you have available to you than it is to have all the tools and not be doing much with them. We're sure you've encountered organisa-tions that have the equivalent of the highest spec car that has all the latest gadgets, yet they don't have anyone on their team who knows how to drive it.

For those who have watched the reality TV shows *Dragons' Den* or *Shark Tank*, you'll often see the investors talk about being focused. Entrepreneurs often get excited about having lots of products; however, this increases choice and dilutes focus.

Rich's take

A beam of sunshine

When I was a child, like many other kids in South Africa, I carried a magnifying glass around with me, not to look at things in great detail but because the sun is really hot and you can use a magnifying glass to concentrate a beam of light to burn a hole in something. The most common target is a leaf, although the odd curtain might have developed a small hole or two as well.

What I, and others, learned very quickly is that if you are impatient and don't focus the lens in place for long enough, then you can't burn a hole through the leaf. It's only by maintaining that focus that you see the outcome you desire. There is often a point where your tiny beam of sunshine doesn't appear to be doing much, then suddenly you see the telltale smoulder and a thin trail of smoke beginning to rise from the leaf. In a business setting, this is about maintaining focus when it comes to initiatives or projects and understanding that it is focus coupled with patience that generally delivers results.

A classic example of this in a business setting is jumping from one new technology to the next without giving each a chance to bed in.

If you are in a business that has a tendency to buy more and more new tools, but that does very little with them (so you're sitting in the bottom right of that grid), your focus has to be on agility. You have to find a way of doing things more quickly because you have all the things you need, but you'll fall behind if you're not using them to maximum effect.

Going back to our preceding diagram, if you're in the top left of that grid, so you don't have all the best tools, then you need to evolve what you have and make it better. You have to adapt so that you can compete. In Formula 1, not all teams are created equal. Some have a much larger budget than others and are able to afford the best tools and personnel. Others have to make do with what they have and find ways to get the most out of what's available to them. A great example of this was the relatively new Formula 1 team Sahara Force India (now known as Racing Point after a takeover) that finished fourth place in the world championships in 2016 and 2017, beating its rivals with a fraction of the budget. The team made the most of the resources available and successfully created one of the biggest upsets in Formula 1.

If you're sitting in the bottom left of that grid, you need to focus on transforming because you have fallen completely behind in that you don't have any of the tools and you're doing very little with what you do have. If you're in this situation, you will have to change the organisation, how it works, and buy all the tools; otherwise, you will never become adaptive.

Look at Meta, Google and Amazon: they are all in the top right of the diagram. They are adaptive organisations and that is where you want to be. The way to get there is to create the right enterprise environment to enable that to happen, which encompasses everything we've talked about so far in this book.

> *"Business is like a heptathlon, with multiple disciplines, distances, skills, and challenges – and you don't need to win them all to win the gold medal. I think the challenge of constantly improving and the excitement of exploring or discovering new areas of opportunity is something that needs to be fed into the culture of the teams within a brand."*
>
> *Aaron Bradley, VP of Technology & Innovation, Wella Company*

Finding your starting point

If you are reading this book and wondering where to start when it comes to transforming into an adaptive enterprise, we have no definitive answer for you. There is no perfect way to go about this. However, there is a framework you can use that will provide a good starting point.

On the right, you can see all the elements we have already covered. You have alignment, which is discussed in Part One. Then you have autonomy and efficiency, which is explored in Part Two. The idea is to make sure everyone is aligned to a common purpose, then use that common purpose to give people autonomy to do the best that they can with what they have control over in order to achieve that purpose. The alignment to the purpose gives you a measurement to keep them on track.

Finally, you have to create an efficient framework within which all of this can take place. Remember the data science example from the previous chapter? There is no point in having highly trained, expensive people if 90% of their time is spent assimilating the data before they can do what you actually need them to, which is the 10%

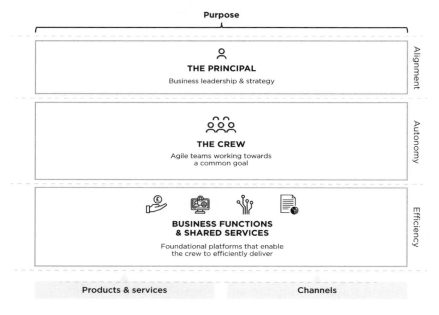

Figure 6.2

of time spent mining it. Efficiency is therefore about the enterprise providing a fertile environment in which autonomy and alignment can function.

This diagram provides a model for how we believe you can make that happen. In addition to those three elements down the right-hand side, there are three key principles to embrace. The first (at the bottom) is moving away from looking at the world through products and channels, and instead looking at the world through the customer.

Step No. 1 is therefore to pivot towards your customer. This is actually a significant shift for many businesses, which typically approach the world from the perspective of having a product and then thinking about whom they are going to sell it to and what channels they are going to use. Instead, start with the customer and build from there. This is the evolution discussed in Chapter 3, where you shift from next best offer and next best action to delivering next best experience for your customers.

Step No. 2 is to create access and ensure there are no bottlenecks to the progress that you are driving in your organisation by delivering efficiency. This is all about lowering the metaphorical walls between the various departments in your organisation, through creating multi-disciplinary agile teams.

Rich's take

What's holding you back?

In the 1990s, I had a company in South Africa and its biggest client at that time was the largest bank in the country. The bank's executives told us they wanted to drive 200 campaigns a week through our engine, up from 10 campaigns at that time, so we carried out an audit of our campaign process and looked at how long it took us to deliver against this requirement.

What we discovered was that we could build a campaign in under an hour, but it took six weeks for a single campaign to get approval from finance, to get the local branch aligned, and to get the product input and marketing data required. Being able to drive that volume of campaigns in that time scale therefore had very little to do with the campaign engine and much more to do with those other areas: finance, product, local branches, and so on.

All of those areas needed to be aligned to lower the walls and make it much easier and quicker for the ball to be passed from one to the other. Only by making those other aspects of the process more efficient would we have had any chance of driving 200 campaigns a week through our engine.

You have to view the shared business services that have to collaborate as potential hurdles to autonomy because if you don't lower the walls between areas like procurement, finance, legal, HR, and so on, you will never achieve autonomy and you won't have the efficiency you need to drive progress.

When it comes to shared services, one of the ways to drive efficiency is making sure that skilled people, such as statisticians, copywriters, designers, and so on, are set up within centres of excellence, where their skills can be drawn on by any of the autonomous teams within the business. What we see all too often is these skilled roles being duplicated across multiple silos, markets, and brands within the business. They provide the same services, but in a very compartmentalised manner. The aim is to use these skilled people as shared resources across the business, because when you are able to do that, the autonomy and alignment we have talked about earlier in the book can start to happen.

Finally, you need to make sure everyone is aligned behind the business' leadership and strategy, which all comes from the principal as we is discussed in Part One. Leaders have to consider how to communicate their vision and strategy to their crew to create the alignment necessary to drive autonomy and efficiency across every part of the organisation.

This is a philosophy that many businesses are looking to embrace and, while this model gives you an overview of what you're aiming for, there will be nuances and challenges within each organisation that need to be addressed.

People make the business

When it comes to processes within organisations changing, it is always worth remembering that every organisation is made of people, and each of these people can respond very differently to certain situations and challenges. It is certainly important to consider how your people can help turn those headwinds into tailwinds, and also to recognise when people might become the headwinds you have to overcome.

Netflix, for example, has the philosophy that it won't tolerate brilliant jerks. That is written into its value statement, which means that it doesn't matter how brilliant you are at what you do, if you don't fit within the organisation and work well with everyone else in that culture, Netflix will objectively support your departure. It is that simple, and this is an important philosophy because it enables the business to stay focused on its purpose and ensure that crucial alignment.

As a team leader, you more than likely have seen how an approach you used in the past with one group of people fell completely flat with a different team. We have to adapt our approach as leaders to a certain degree, and that is all part of playing a role within an adaptive organisation.

In addition to remembering that businesses are made of people, you also have to remember that how those people work and respond in different situations will be out of your control to a certain degree. You haven't been involved in every step of their personal development, so you have to accept that they might do things differently than you do. This circles back around to the concept of autonomy, and highlights why it's so important that each person on a team has some degree of freedom in how she approaches her work.

If we bring this all the way back to the fact that you want to develop human-centric relationships and behaviours for your customers, you have to start with people, and that actually means starting with the people within your business. As Richard Branson said, "You can't do a good business with a bad person. Find the right people to work with and you can't go wrong."

"I believe that people are motivated most by other people – whether it's through in-depth conversations or simply through off-the-cuff comments shared in fleeting chats. People want to contribute thoughts and ideas, and feel they are playing their part in the conversation, a social moment, or a new idea. Whether we realise it or not, at different times of day and in different situations, we're all inspiring and motivating those around us."

Benjamin Braun, CMO, Samsung

Highlights

Businesses operate across multiple shades of grey in the modern world. Just as there is no single "right" strategy, there is also no perfect way of building and developing an adaptive organisation. There are, however, certain traits that you will see across all adaptive organisations; namely, alignment at every level with the overall vision and purpose of the organisation, autonomy within teams that allows people to work to the best of their abilities, and efficiency at every level of a business.

All businesses will encounter headwinds at certain times, and the key is to find a way to use what you have to turn those headwinds into tailwinds that propel you forwards rather than pushing you back. As we have seen through the COVID-19 pandemic, crises can present great opportunities for organisations that are able to pivot, adapt, and embrace change.

The concept of headwinds and tailwinds is one that is very familiar in Formula 1, where teams experience literal headwinds as their respective car is physically ploughing through a wall of resistance. One of the ways the teams deal with this is through the aerodynamics of the car to neutralise the forward flow of air and thereby minimise the drag and maximise momentum. Simply reducing forward resistance can help with the direction of travel and give a team the edge over its competitors. If you can get close enough to the car ahead (on the straight), then you have less work to do to overcome this resistance and you effectively turn that headwind into a tailwind. This is called the slipstream, and if you can turn resistance into slipstream, swap a headwind for a tailwind, then you're on course for the chequered flag.

Chapter 7
It Will Rain on Your Parade
Mitigating and adapting to events beyond your control

"Only when the tide goes out do you see who has been swimming naked."

– Warren Buffett

Picture the scene. You're on a family holiday in a seaside resort in England. We all know it's always a gamble with the weather – will you get a week of glorious sunshine and warm temperatures, enjoying sunny days at the beach where the biggest worry is how long you'll have to queue to buy the kids ice cream? Or will you keep getting caught in deluges and spend your days huddled behind a windbreak at the beach, wrapped in towels and all the clothing you took with you while the kids race in and out of the sea before eventually getting cold?

Az grew up in a seaside town, and his first job was working in Britain's largest joke shop. For this shop, the holiday season was crucial, a time when it had the large majority of its business. Of course, just like those on holiday, the one thing this business couldn't control was the weather.

Let's go back to your family at the beach. You're huddled behind a windbreak and there are threatening grey clouds building on the horizon. Eventually, you give up and bundle the kids back to the car just as it starts to rain. You're camping, so the prospect of going back to the campsite and hiding in the tent isn't overly appealing. Instead you decide to wander into the town and browse in the shops. This is what the majority of other holidaymakers have decided to do too.

At the joke shop, business picks up dramatically when it rains. Everyone tries to find shelter and that increases footfall in the shop, which of course also increases sales. You walk in and the kids' eyes light up at the rows and rows of toys, pranks, and other props lining the shop's shelves. You can see them working out how much holiday money they have to spend here and you sigh. At least it's dry though, so if the kids want to browse for half an hour you're not going to stop them. You glance around the shop, seeing rows of whoopee cushions, hand buzzers, goo in a multitude of colours, and a range of magic tricks lining the shelves. You had hoped there might be some umbrellas tucked away somewhere, but apparently they don't hold enough comedy value.

However, the lack of umbrellas isn't due to their practical and unfunny nature. The shop that Az worked at made one crucial observation about people's shopping and browsing behaviour when it rained; the owner noticed that if he sold umbrellas people would pop in, pick up an umbrella and head back out into the rain. As a result, he stopped stocking umbrellas, so that the people who came into the store would stay longer and usually spend more money.

Even though the owner of the shop couldn't control when it was going to rain, he could control the circumstances in his store when it did.

The point is: It will rain on your parade, things will always go wrong but, as a business, the key is in how you adapt and react when things go wrong. A lot of businesses try to mitigate all of the challenges upfront and, as a result, they carry out a lot of analysis which can result in analysis paralysis.

No matter how much analysis you carry out though, there will always be things outside of your control and you can't predict everything that is going to happen. What you have to think about is how you manage or adapt around the things that are out of your control. This is where agile and adaptive organisations really come into their own because they are able to change their approach when it rains on their parade.

This principle of business adaptation really came to the fore with the COVID-19 pandemic. As Warren Buffett's quote at the beginning of this chapter points out: When the tide goes out, you can see who has been swimming naked. The tide has just gone a really long way out in the business world, and we have seen plenty of businesses that were exposed suddenly rushing to get a towel, racing back into the sea, or just standing in the shallows hoping no one notices.

Being able to adapt to your environment is crucial, but it is especially important during times of crisis. This is also when you have to play to your strengths.

"History tells us that periods of significant adversity can foster challenges but also innovation on a grand scale. Those leaders that can find the balance between critical short-term needs and aspirational long-term vision will set their business on a new trajectory that will propel them forward and guide team members along the journey."

Paul Robson, President of Adobe International, Adobe

A great example of adaptation to an external environment came in the final race of the 2008 Formula 1 season, when Lewis Hamilton needed a fifth-place finish to claim his first world championship title. The conditions at the Brazilian grand prix were highly changeable, with drizzle and eventually heavy rain arriving towards the end of the race.

This was when Hamilton's McLaren/Mercedes team brought him into the pit to change his tyres from dry to intermediates, as did the other frontrunners for the race. However, Toyota's Timo Glock chose to persevere on dry tyres in the drizzle. In the final lap, with Glock in fifth place and Hamilton chasing him down from sixth, the rain intensified. This gave Hamilton an opportunity to close the gap and overtake Glock on the final corner of the race to claim fifth place and just enough points to take the championship from race winner Felipe Massa.

Hamilton is renowned for being a strong driver in wet conditions, and his team knew that. The team members adapted their strategy to allow him to play to his strengths, and this decision, coupled with Hamilton's abilities, enabled him to adapt to the environment and use it to his advantage.

Flexible strategies are a necessity

We have said many times in this book that, as a business, you need to have multiple strategies. However, you also need to accept that no matter how many strategies you have, it will rain somewhere on your parade and you have to consider how you will respond to that and have the flexibility to respond when the unexpected happens.

In Formula 1, there are some tracks where the rain can be incredibly localised, in that it will be raining on one-third of the track and dry elsewhere. In this situation, the principal and race teams have to decide whether they go for the strategy that sees them do well on the two-thirds of the track that's dry, and hope that they survive on the wet third, or whether they go for the reverse.

What we're getting at is that it's not always rain or no rain. Sometimes there will be a bit of rain mixed in with dry spells and thundery showers, and all you can do is respond to those changing conditions.

If you look at Formula 1 teams in those situations, they don't all take the same strategy. Some will take a riskier strategy because they are confident they can use the adversity to get ahead of their competitors. This is another aspect of it raining on your parade: Do you drown in the floods or do use the water to float ahead?

Not all businesses are created equal

Regardless of the industry you operate in, you will be part of the same broader environment as every other business. Even though we're often in the same storm, we're not all in the same boat. This means that even though industries and the businesses within them might appear very different if you compare them, they are often experiencing similar challenges.

It can also be very easy to look at industries in terms of the threats and opportunities that they have as well as to identify the common challenges businesses operating in a specific industry are likely to face. However, there is another way that we categorise businesses outside of their standard industry verticals, which is as indirect, term, and frequent organisations. This allows us to identify those common challenges that transcend industries.

Indirect organisations are ones that don't have a direct relationship with the end customer. Normally their products or services will reach the customer through an intermediary of some sort. Businesses classed as FMCG, CPG, Media & Entertainment, and so on would fall under this category.

Term organisations are businesses that start with a single purchase moment but have a service relationship over time. Examples would be automotive, utilities, telecommunications, and so on. For these organisations, there will often be a renewal at some point so creating that long-term relationship with the customer is key.

Frequent organisations are what we describe as standard retailers, where customers make quick and frequent purchases.

These categories apply across multiple industries and, depending on which of these three categories your organisation falls under, some of your behaviours will shift accordingly. Looking at your business in this way allows you to draw comparisons in what might otherwise seem like unlikely places.

Brands that fall into the indirect category are providing a product but it is going to someone else's customer, so the brand doesn't always know who is consuming its products. As soon as you step into the term and frequent categories, it doesn't matter whose product you're selling anymore because you are selling to *your* customer. This is why Amazon can sell almost anything to almost anybody because it has the customer base. If your organisation is in the indirect category, you have to work much harder to know who is buying your product.

These categories look at businesses by the relationship they have with their customers rather than by industry verticals. What we've seen during the COVID-19 pandemic are businesses like Deliveroo, thinking creatively and diversifying in terms of how it produces and delivers its products, and sells to consumers.

For example, the last year has seen the trend of dark kitchens, which was already gathering momentum before the pandemic, accelerating. Dark kitchens can be located anywhere, which means there is no longer any need for expensive real estate, such as in fancy restaurants. You can produce amazing food from an industrial estate and, because so many people are now ordering in, it's how fast you get it that matters rather than where it is produced.

As well as reducing the cost of the real estate for that dark kitchen, there are reduced production and staffing costs.

One of the principles we want to get across here is that your vertical can't protect you. It is your business model that might be under threat. You can't use your industry to shelter from the expectations of your consumers.

Follow the leader or lead the pack?

While writing this book, we were involved in a call with a client about a very novel idea around brand alignment and personal alignment. This is a very new concept, which we're expecting to be big in about a year's time. During the course of that call, one of the people involved said that the client wanted to see where this had been done before. The person asked us for case studies and to find out where it had worked in the past, which of course we can't provide because it is a novel concept.

About 10 minutes later in that same call, the same person told us that the client is a very visionary business that wants to establish itself as tech leaders in its space. There is a significant disconnect between those two concepts.

On the one hand, this client is saying it doesn't want to do anything new unless somebody else has done it first and it's worked, and on the other hand, it's saying it wants to lead the way and be a tech leader. Those two things are completely incongruent and therein lies the challenge.

If the client is clear about its purpose and know what it is measuring, it won't need to see what anyone else has done; it will simply need to decide whether this is the right thing for it to do and if the answer is "Yes", to just do it.

If you're not able to link what you're doing to the outcome it's going to drive, then you are in the eye of the storm with no compass to navigate to safety through the driving rain and howling winds. However, if you have a compass (in business the ability to link what you're doing to the outcome), then the answer becomes clear and you have a clear pathway out of the metaphorical storm. This all comes back to what is discussed in Part One, where the principal sets a clear direction of travel for the organisation. From there, you move to Part Two, where there is alignment within the crew. If you have autonomous teams and you know what you are doing, then the decision is clear.

Being able to connect the dots and link the outcomes to what you're doing doesn't only apply when you are examining fears within a business, but is also important when it comes to beliefs or ortho-doxies within a business. Linking the beliefs within your business to the outcomes will dictate whether those beliefs are true. If you can't link a belief to an outcome, it isn't true and you need to evaluate it.

When you are making new decisions within your business, you will feel fear, but you have to do it anyway. What guides you to the right decisions in a given situation is your purpose and clarity about what you are trying to achieve.

A constant process of evolution

One area that requires decisions to be made frequently is in technology; it is continuously changing and that has a big impact on businesses in every industry. What you, as a business, have to do is work out how you can adapt around this landscape of ever-evolving technology.

Kodak is an example of a business that completely misread the technological landscape and how it would evolve. Did you know that Kodak invented the digital camera in 1974? However, the company didn't release it because they were convinced that the concept wouldn't catch on. They were working on the belief that consumers wanted to hold physical photographs and wouldn't engage with pictures in a digital format.

Rich's take

The elephant versus the rhino

I can tell you from experience that when an African elephant charges you, it's terrifying. However, when you're seeing it on the television or at a distance, it's almost amusing because it's the only animal that never has all four of its legs off the ground at the same time. When you see it running, it's hard not to laugh at its almost comical waddle.

Although I joke, it is still scary when an elephant is charging you because it's stamping its feet, flapping its ears, and making lots of noise. But in doing this, it is giving you lots of opportunity to get out of the way. You will see and hear it coming.

The brown rhino, on the other hand, hides in the bush and by the time you see it coming there is no running away. When the rhino steps out of the bush and out of its cover, you're screwed, basically. The point of this story is that if you can see your competitors lumbering across the plain at 15 miles per hour towards you, they are not the ones you have to worry about. It's the ones you don't see coming that you have to watch out for. Those are the ones that will rain on your parade and those are the ones you have to be able to respond to very quickly.

This is all about adaptability, responsiveness, and continually sensing and being aware of what's going on around you. As an organisation you have to be able to respond and make quick decisions, you can't wait for someone else to tell you that it's okay to do something. You can't see the rhinos, so you have to be able to adapt and respond quickly, all while keeping an eye on the elephants so you can course correct away from them in plenty of time.

Don't turn the elephant into a rhino

The other thing to be aware of is that you can turn an elephant into a rhino. If you look at the financial services sector, traditional banks and institutions haven't evolved for decades. They saw new organisations like Monzo and Starling coming into the picture, but they didn't course correct in time and begin their transformations.

The new banks have accelerated what they're doing and now the traditional banks have accelerated what they have needed to do for years, which has brought them to the point of transformation.

In this instance, transformation is getting those traditional institutions to the point at which they can catch up. However, had they accelerated their efforts to be customer first in terms of their own outcomes, they may have been closer to keeping up with what consumers wanted and the changes that were coming down the track, and could even have preempted some of those things. All of this may have given them a head start on the rhino.

There is also an element of talent versus hard work at play here, and not only in the financial sector. Businesses, and the people within them, can become complacent or be afraid of stepping out of their comfort zones. However, people can learn new skills just as businesses can build new capabilities. What enables that to happen is the character and culture within an organisation, and this is what's important.

People often rely on what they've done before and value that experience over what they could do for the business in the future. It's the organisations and people who say "This is how we've always done it" that are most at risk of being hit by the brown rhino.

It's not only in the finance sector where this has been an issue. Just look at what happened in ecommerce in the early months of the COVID-19 pandemic. As is noted in Chapter 6, many businesses suddenly made decisions because of the crisis. What you have to learn to do is make those decisions without needing a crisis to force you to take that leap.

There was one case study from Shopify that typified that period. Lindt launched an ecommerce site in five days in 2020. If you had asked any organisation before the pandemic, it would have told you that it would take 12 months to two years, minimum, to get an ecommerce site live. This example just goes to show that if you make quick decisions, and you make the right decisions, you have the ability to evolve over time and that can make a huge difference to the success of your business.

"During the height of the pandemic lockdown, in-store footfall across Europe was down by almost half. Forward-thinking brands began to rapidly move their expertise online to survive. Almost overnight, a company website was more than just a shop window. It became the only open shop."

Benjamin Braun, CMO, Samsung

Slipstreaming and overtaking

As a business, you need to put yourself in a position where you can make those quick decisions, even if you are trailing your competitors. The concept of slipstreaming is well-known in motorsports, where a driver is able to keep pace with the car in front by staying in its slipstream, an area just behind the moving vehicle where the air is moving at a similar rate to the vehicle itself.

In business, there are two ways to use a slipstream. One is to help you keep pace with the leader in your field and, while you might not be able to edge ahead of them just by staying in their slipstream, you will be able to keep your other competitors at bay.

The other opportunity that arises from a slipstream is to slingshot. You can see this concept in the movie *Days of Thunder,* where Tom Cruise's character Cole Trickle uses a slingshot manoeuvre to overtake rival driver Rowdy Burns to win his first NASCAR race. The idea of a slingshot is to use the momentum gained in the slipstream to propel your vehicle around the one you have been following.

An example of a business that used the slingshot approach was LoveFilm, an organisation that started in the slipstream of traditional movie rentals by providing unlimited postal DVD rentals to customers. It evolved its business model to online streaming and, after being acquired by Amazon, it pivoted its business model to be a competitor to Netflix by creating its own exclusive content. In two steps, it was able to slingshot from following Blockbuster to being competitive with Netflix.

This links back into what is discussed in Chapter 4 and making all your shots count. In business, when you see a competitor take a shot, you can use that as an opportunity to gauge the market and then make a better shot. You're using that competitor's momentum to propel your own organisation further forward.

Creating opportunities in a crisis

With hindsight, the General Data Protection Regulation (GDPR) has presented opportunities, but at the time it was a crisis for most businesses. We often see incredible opportunities emerging from crisis situations and, in many cases, it is taking these opportunities that allows a business to slingshot around its competitors.

When it comes to turning headwinds into tailwinds, COVID-19 provides numerous examples where businesses were able to make decisions very quickly to either turn the situation to their advantage or, at the very least, to ensure they didn't fall behind.

During the first three months of the global pandemic, the ecommerce sector experienced 10 years' worth of growth. It's quite likely that most businesses that launched ecommerce solutions in that period had proposals to do so in the pipeline, but due to internal restrictions until that point, they had been stuck. All of a sudden, the COVID-19 pandemic comes along and those proposals fly through.

"It is critical to highlight and recognise how the global impact of COVID-19 has dramatically driven changes around online consumer behaviour .... On a recurring basis, we have seen transformational online experience development to meet this step-change in online activity. Investment in online that previously has taken years has accelerated to just months or quarters."

Nicholas Cumisky, YouTube

The hidden benefit from such a crisis can be the realisation that businesses have not been able to make decisions at the pace required to stay ahead, and to build a muscle that can respond to change.

Where are you sitting?

We've been working with LNER (a national rail organisation in the UK) and in a recent industry presentation that they shared, explained how they have added a simple piece of functionality to its website in the last year that has made a significant difference to its booking experience. That simple piece of functionality is allowing customers to choose their seats on the train when they book their tickets.

This is a piece of functionality that some people within that business have been wanting to add for some time, but it was deprioritised because it was difficult to quantify what the value would be in comparison to other features. As soon as COVID-19 came along, they implemented it and, as it turns out, it has had a positive effect for the business.

Crisis opportunity trickles down through a business from large decisions to small decisions, and sometimes it can be the small decisions that make the greatest difference.

However, the problem is you can't rely on a crisis to make decisions, and the challenge we see many businesses facing is that they lock down their decision making process too much because they are so scared of making the wrong decision. Jeff Bezos once said, "If you think it's going to be expensive to make the wrong decision, wait until you see what it costs to make no decision."

We saw this paralysis in the face of decision making in some businesses around the implementation of the GDPR legislation. Many companies were slow to get their GDPR compliance in order and then six months before it came into force, they entered panic mode. This was then heightened when large fines started being handed out for noncompliance. It went from being a nice-to-have to a business priority very quickly.

One of the difficulties when you're making decisions from a place of crisis, however, is that it can be easy to make the wrong decisions in your haste to make any decision. Organisations can spend a lot of time looking for a solution without ever fully understanding what the problem is or without making any effort to understand the problem.

The result of this is that they often jump on what other organisations have seen as a solution, often spending significant amounts of money on technology that is never going to add value and that is, in reality, an unwise decision.

We saw a very simple example of this with the cookie compliance statements and tracking when GDPR came into force. Due to the unknown nature of how the legislation would be enforced, the early adopters stopped tracking completely, and everyone else followed in their footsteps. However, when these organisations realised that they no longer had insights running through the business due to the huge holes this approach had created in their data, businesses started to understand that the real problem wasn't about tracking, but about the ethical use of tracking through the lens of consumer privacy. This shift in understanding resulted in businesses looking at better solutions that worked for everyone by providing the data they needed without infringing a consumer's privacy – in effect, a fair exchange because it's value for data.

In the small percentage of businesses that do start to think about the problem, rather than instantly seeking a solution, the vast majority don't stop to think about whether they are asking the right question in the first place. Those that seek to understand the problem and aren't afraid to ask very different questions are disruptors. These businesses seek to understand what their customers need, almost certainly look at what everyone else is doing, and then do what they believe is right.

Change beyond a crisis

As we said, you can't wait for a crisis to create opportunities or force transformation, but you need the capacity to adapt to a crisis when such a situation arises. We have seen some businesses fail during the COVID-19 pandemic and we have also seen some businesses change and pivot very effectively during this period of significant disruption. While some organisations won't have considered that change beyond the context of COVID, those that are adaptive will stand out because of their ability to pivot and walk that fine line between what they were doing before and what they need to do now to survive.

The challenge, particularly for well-established businesses, is that they have spent probably the last 40 or 50 years battening down the hatches around total quality management. In the West, the arguably restrictive processes many businesses developed were in response to the superior quality of the products coming out of Japan in the late 1970s and 1980s. These processes have evolved to the point where they're not designed to allow flexibility or autonomy, both of which are key attributes of an adaptive organisation.

For older organisations, therein lies the challenge. These processes have evolved over decades and it is therefore difficult to change them quickly, but there is a need to change quickly in order to continue to compete.

You can't fight modernisation

Modernisation happens, and you can choose to embrace it and evolve or fight it and become obsolete. Look at the samurai in the nineteenth century[1]. They went from being elite warriors to an obsolete fighting force in a matter of decades as a result of the modernisation of warfare that was introduced by the Europeans and Americans who were attempting to colonise Japan.

---

[1] https://daily.jstor.org/whatever-happened-to-the-samurai/

The Americans, in particular, used their superior weaponry to force Japan to open its borders to trade, and this led to a period of modernisation for the samurai army and navy. They used the samurai principles and adopted western weapons to evolve. While on the one hand, you could argue this made the traditional samurai obsolete, on the other, you could describe this as an evolution of the Japanese fighting force.

What this demonstrates is that new technologies will come along, no matter how hard you try to fight against them. The Japanese closed their borders to trade with Europe and America in all but a few select ports for decades in a bid to preserve their way of life but, in the end, they were forced to modernise and evolve.

Economic upheaval: adapt or die

In the preceding example, the samurai chose to adapt, even though it meant a significant change to their way of life and how they fought. Japan also adapted to the influx of foreign trade, shifting away from its isolationist approach. While this was in the era pre-globalisation when national economies tended to function independently of one another, it was still a significant change for Japan. These days, as we know, an economic shock in one nation can ricochet around the world very quickly.

The COVID-19 pandemic was a very recent example of how the global economy can change very quickly, and businesses have to adapt just as quickly to keep up. There are countless stories from this period of businesses struggling, just as there are plenty of businesses performing exceptionally well.

We have an FMCG client that landed on the exceptional performance side of the spectrum. We had many clients who were cutting back on their marketing because they were struggling, while this client decided to cut back on its marketing because it was doing so well and couldn't fulfil orders for its stock. Baby milk was one of the core products that this client couldn't manufacture fast enough to keep up with demand. The business had to adapt to the situation and work out how it could maintain its service even if it couldn't deliver to the scale of the demand, and one of those decisions was to reduce its marketing spend.

During the pandemic, we saw restaurants turning into takeaways, offering home meal kit deliveries, and even fresh produce deliveries. A local flour mill near Rich started selling flour directly to consumers in 16 kg bags and even offered home sour dough kits. There were hundreds of amazing stories of innovation and inspired thinking where businesses rapidly pivoted and adapted to cope with a situation that no one saw coming.

Turning motion into progress

When your organisation is facing situations outside of its control, such as events that are happening within the economy, what will affect your ability to turn motion into progress is the answers to the following three questions, all of which we have explored in great detail earlier in this book:

1. Have leaders defined (principal) a very clear direction for your organisation, and do you and everybody else at your organisation know what direction that is?

2. Is your organisation empowered and functioning efficiently in terms of its teamwork (crew), and are you measuring the right outputs?

3. Are you geared up to understand how these things in the environment (season) are going to affect you? Can you mitigate for them, change them to your advantage, and respond at the pace required?

That third answer is crucial because you need to know which of the events outside of your control will affect you in order to know how and when you need to adapt. Understanding whether these things will affect your organisation comes back to measurement. If you measure what matters, as is discussed in Chapter 2, you will know whether those events are going to affect you.

If something will affect your business, feel the fear and respond because if you wait you will fall even further behind. Don't become the rabbit in the headlights that is paralysed and fails to make any decision. In many instances, it can be better to make the wrong decision and course correct later than it is to make no decision.

In his book *21 Lessons for the 21st Century*,[2] Yuval Harari explained that, for the first time ever, the past is probably no longer a safe predictor for the future. If you consider this on a personal level, you have probably always considered your parents to be a safe haven and would go to your parents for advice because they had seen it all before and would be the voice of reason to help you make a decision for the future. However, Harari suggests that your parents are now the wrong people to ask because they haven't seen this future and they have no idea where it is going.

In business, the same concept applies. For a lot of the challenges organisations are facing, the past is no longer a precedent. Instead, as a business, you need to understand your capabilities, understand what you are trying to achieve and be clear on your purpose, know your people, and, even if you feel fearful about a decision, you have to make it anyway.

When the rain is lashing down on a Formula 1 track, the danger levels increase significantly and, no doubt, there is an element of fear amongst the team; but those who see the opportunity in this situation, and decide to adapt their race strategy to take advantage of this, are the ones who end up on the podium.

---

[2]Yuval Noah Harari, *21 Lessons for the 21st Century*, Vintage (22 August 2019)

While the uncertainty over the future might create fear, it is also an incredible opportunity, particularly for organisations that have been stuck in their ways for so long, to reset. You can use some of these changes that are happening in the economy or within your industry to press the reset button, change the old ways, and really focus on what you're trying to achieve. What outcome do you want?

You have to always ask: "Does this affect the business?" If the answer to that question is "No", you should be getting rid of it. If the answer is "Yes", ask whether you are doing the right thing and, if you're not, set out the steps you need to take to make sure you are doing the right thing.

Where do you start?

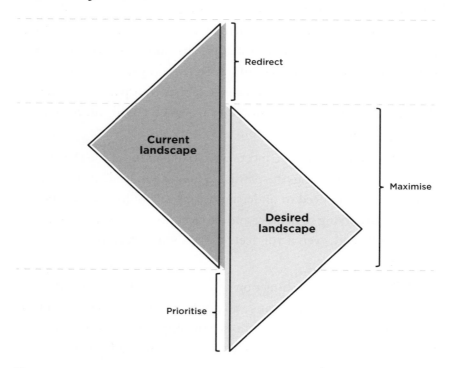

Figure 7.1

The preceding diagram outlines an approach to find your starting point. The triangle on the left of that diagram is your current landscape and the triangle on the right is your future landscape. Where those triangles meet is where current and future landscapes are aligned. You have to accelerate anything that falls into that area and use what is completely aligned to your best advantage.

The space in the top right is where your current landscape doesn't match your future landscape and these are things that aren't going to align with your direction of travel. You have to kill these things very quickly to prevent them from holding you back. The space at the bottom left represents where your future isn't aligned to your current. This is where you need a very clear strategy to close the gap by building processes and strategies that will get you to where you want to be in the future.

The three key takeaways here are to maximise what you already have that is working towards the future you want; to kill anything that is dragging you backwards and further away from your future; and to make sure you have the processes and capabilities in place to build what you're going to need to meet your future landscape.

Stuck in a cycle

There are many examples of organisations that are slow to kill off projects in that top corner of the diagram. A large multinational decided around four years ago that it needed to get a data management platform (DMP). Around 2015/2016, this

(continued)

(continued)

was a piece of technology that everyone felt was a must-have. Even businesses that didn't require a DMP bought one, although they didn't always get the desired value from it.

This particular business jumped on the bandwagon and started the process of building a DMP. The organisation went for a "think big, go big" approach, creating a DMP for every market and across every one of its brands. That meant it took 3.5 years to build the business case and choose the technology. By the time the company had done this, DMPs were becoming less relevant due to the launch of the customer data platform (CDP), which meant many businesses had moved on from DMPs and were focusing elsewhere. As a result of this change in the market, the company shelved the project and is now preparing a global tender for a CDP. This is a great example of Groundhog Day.

Many organisations get stuck in a similar cycle. They are doing okay in that middle section of the diagram, but they are not able to kill the top fast enough and move to the bottom. As a result, they end up in this cycle of wasted effort and money. They are going around in circles and never progressing forwards.

The challenge often is that businesses don't want to be seen to have moved in the wrong direction or to have wasted money on projects before they got off the ground, which means they persevere longer than they should. In most cases, this, of course, means they end up wasting more money. Sometimes you need to take the bold decision and kill a project early to save money in the long term.

Az's take

When the chips are down

I meet up with a group of my friends around once a year for a poker game. It's a £20 buy-in and the winner takes the pot, so it's not a high-stakes game but it's enough that it means something.

The last time we were all playing poker together, I had a reasonable hand and ended up in the last two in the game. I wasn't sure what my friend had, so I decided to go in with some confidence and put 400 chips down, which for the size of our pot was a medium level of bet. I saw my friend waver, and then he matched my 400. So I put 400 down again. He matched. I did it again, and again he matched. This continued a couple more times until my friend faltered.

He said, "That was absolutely brilliant. You've just wound me in and now I don't know what to do because I've gone so far down that route I either have to fold and lose everything, or I have to keep going and hope I'm calling a bluff."

This is what many businesses do with the kinds of technology projects we just talked about. They get so far down the line that they become afraid to pull out. The decision maker needs to kill projects like that and cut the company's losses sooner.

As is noted in Chapter 2, many businesses have processes geared around starting projects, but they don't have processes geared around closing them. There is always this temptation to "just spend £1 million more", thinking that this will be enough to complete the project, but when something is already running massively over budget and you can't measure the contribution to your goal, you have to stop and not spend a penny more.

Escaping the headlights

This all comes back to that Jeff Bezos quote we shared earlier, "If you think it's going to be expensive to make the wrong decision, wait until you see what it costs to make no decision." However, when it comes to complex topics such as GDPR and Brexit, there are so many grey areas it is easy to see how businesses become trapped in the metaphorical headlights.

This fear of making the wrong decision is what holds back many organisations. Decisions have to be made at some point and, the longer you leave it to make a decision, the more likely you are to make a decision from a place of fear, which typically means logic goes out of the window.

Rich's take

Are you drowning?

Surfing is a popular pastime in South Africa, where I'm from, and, as a result, I am a qualified lifesaver. I remember when I completed my life-saving course that I was taught the biggest danger when you swim out to rescue someone who is drowning is that the victim will drown you.

You can picture the scene: the person is scared and struggling, and as soon as he sees you he latches onto you because he is so desperate to be saved. However, in his desperation, he ends up drowning both of you.

Business can face a similar situation. An organisation becomes so scared of making the wrong decision that as soon as something that looks like a saviour appears (and often it's a piece of technology), it latches onto this saviour and throws its lot in with what it hopes is the solution. The organisation becomes so desperate for an answer that it goes all-in when it sees someone else doing something that *looks* like the answer.

This is why so many organisations get trapped in a pattern of making the wrong decisions, often thinking that technology will solve their problems when the reality is that the problem is much bigger than technology.

You don't always need a saviour

We also have a friend who used to work as a lifeguard. One day, we saw a boat out at sea and all the people on board were waving frantically at the shore. After watching for a few moments, he decided they needed help and, instead of calling the coast guard, he decided it would be better to swim out to them. However, around halfway to the boat, he realised he hadn't accounted for the tide and therefore he got swept farther away from the boat.

We were watching this from the shore and, understandably, getting worried, so we called the coast guard, which safely collected him. The irony was that the family on the boat weren't in trouble at all, they were just enthusiastically waving to the people on the shore.

This illustrates the point that sometimes a business doesn't need a saviour to come along. You may be able to make do with what you have or make better decisions. To make better decisions, it's important to look at the bigger picture and explore the situation from the perspective of others, both in the business world and among your customers.

What's happening in the consumers' world?

As a business, you can't control the economy, but it's important to remember that what is happening within the economy affects your consumers as much as it affects your organisation. If we take the COVID-19 pandemic as an example again. One of the reasons for this trend that was identified during 2020 was an increase in stock market activity among individual investors, using platforms like Robin Hood. The reason for this trend was that lots of people in the UK were furloughed and therefore had not only the time to explore investing, but, in many cases, more disposable income than usual.

It was a similar story in the US, where many people received $1 000 stimulus cheques during the pandemic and, for those who didn't need the money immediately, investing it in the stock market was a popular option.

Elections can also have an impact on consumer behaviour. In the UK, Brexit has obviously been a challenge that businesses have had to navigate. In our organisation, we have had to consider the impact of Brexit on conversion rates across currencies as well as on our own teams and people within the business.

All of these national and international events can have an impact on both your business and your consumers, so you have to think about how you will respond to these and adapt accordingly.

You can't control your customers

While you need to be aware of how different events are impacting your customers, you also need to know your limitations in terms of what you can control. Chapter 3 talks about the concept of inbound, outbound, and unbound interactions with customers. When it comes to your customers, the only thing you can control is your interactions with them, but there will be so much more to your customers' interactions with your brand than the ones you have control over.

In terms of the season, and the elements that are outside of your control, it is the unbound interactions that are crucial. Chapter 3 discusses these in the context of a bank providing a mortgage, but having no opportunity to affect the interactions with the customer's solicitor, estate agent, surveyor, and so on.

When we consider unbound interactions from an organisational perspective, it branches into areas such as consumer trends. This could be veganism, sustainability, the push to reduce sugar in certain products. All of these trends can have a huge impact on your organisation, but they aren't necessarily things you will have foreseen or they might be trends that have gained greater momentum among consumers than you expected. You need to embrace listening to the voice of your customers and, more importantly, amplify what they say to fully understand their needs and expectations.

"My mother is 80 years old, and a year and a half before the pandemic she asked me whether she would be able to use an iPad if she bought one, which I always thought would be a challenge given that whenever she visited me I would tape up the remote control so that she could only access the power button, channel buttons, and volume control.

In 2020, my mother was living in New York City. I rented her a home 500 yards down the road from mine in Connecticut because I didn't want her in the city with the pandemic raging, and it meant I could visit her every evening. A month and a half into her time living in that house, I'd walk in and find her on a

Zoom call or on Facebook or Instagram. She was getting TikTok videos from my daughter. She was ordering all her products from Amazon Prime, using Fresh Direct, and getting annoyed with Bed Bath & Beyond because they weren't giving her good service.

I remember thinking one day, 'How did this happen?' She went from being someone who had to ask me if she could operate an iPad to a digitally savvy consumer. That's the challenge for businesses now, not only has the consumer changed, but so too has the consumer expectation."

Craig Dempster, Global CEO, Merkle

Expectations versus reality

As Craig notes, consumers and their expectations have shifted considerably across all demographics since the pandemic in 2020. The challenge for brands is keeping up with this change and making sure that consumer expectations are met or exceeded.

As an example where expectations don't match up to reality, you can watch the Jim Carey film *Bruce Almighty*. The premise of that movie is that Jim Carey's character becomes omnipotent and thinks he's going to have a wonderful time with the power of God. He does all the fun stuff, but he neglects his responsibilities and there are then consequences as a result.

Think about that experience in the context of a customers, and the amount of times customers have had an experience with a brand that hasn't met their expectations all because a brand promises to delight and then falls short. As a brand, you are always going to be benchmarked against that experience.

In an interview many years ago, Steve Jobs said that customers don't measure the quality of a product based on what they see or hear in an advert; they measure quality based on the product and its performance. He made this comment at a time when Japanese companies were known for producing quality products, but American companies weren't. He observed that the Japanese brands never mentioned quality in their advertising because they knew that customers would judge the quality based on what they received, not on what they had been told.

Az's take

Getting hooked

At the risk of sounding a little corny, I can still remember the first time I used an iPhone, down to where I was and even how I was sitting because that moment resonated so well. A friend and colleague of mine was one of the hundreds of people who queued up to buy the first iPhone on its release. I hadn't bought into the hype and couldn't understand his desire to queue for a phone.

I was heading up the UX and performance team at the time, and my friend brought his new iPhone into work and got everyone on our team to take a look. I distinctly remember him calling me over to try it because I hadn't rushed across to his desk. I knelt down by his desk, which was just behind mine, and he handed me the phone.

My expectation was that it would be similar to the previous phones I had owned to this point – namely, slightly resistant and clunky to touch. I swiped the screen and it gave

(continued)

(continued)

me the "wow" feeling. That one moment changed my expectations of user interface design forever. The smoothness and reactiveness of the touchscreen and the soft finishes combined with the way the screen bounced made it feel real, even though there was no physical feedback. I bought one as soon as the phones came back in stock. I was sold. Apple did everything right and then launched its product at the right time.

This is all about the experience customers have with your brand. However, how they measure that experience will be based on the expectations you have set prior to that experience or interaction. One of the reasons Az had such a "wow" moment with the iPhone is that he had low expectations, based on his experiences with other brands. That worked in Apple's favour when he used the iPhone because this made it really stand out.

As another example, Az read *The Lost World: Jurassic Park* before the movie was released, only to not enjoy the film because it wasn't accurate to the book. (He's vowed never again to read a book before watching a movie adaptation.) His expectations were not met by the reality. That's not to say there aren't very successful movies that have been adapted from books.

Take the *Harry Potter* series, which has performed phenomenally well as a movie series. One of the reasons these adaptations have been so well received is that JK Rowling was closely involved in the making of the film, which helped to align viewers' expectations with what they saw on the screen.

As a brand, you are looking to hit this sweet spot, one where your customers' needs align with what you provide.

Meeting customer needs is your best competitive advantage

The final element that is outside of your control is your competitors. You can't control what they do or don't do, but meeting your customers' needs gives you the best competitive advantage because it means you are always the most relevant at that given moment in time. Look at the example Az shared about his first iPhone experience. Apple met his needs and exceeded his expectations, which meant he became an iPhone user.

This is about the moments, experiences, and relationships you have with your customers. Each interaction is made up of many moments. Think back to the concept of the Fluid Cube that is shared in Chapter 3. Customers are not one-dimensional, any more than your interactions with them are. You have to be able to adapt to your customer's changing needs and to understand that those needs can shift within the course of an interaction or series of interactions.

"People can be made aware of a product and purchase in just a matter of seconds. And this presents a real opportunity for brands to be meaningfully present in the spaces their customers are now occupying."

Nicola Mendelsohn, CBE, VP GBG, Meta

If you think about this in the context of sport, you can train and analyse your opposition as much as you want, but on the day of the match or race, anything can happen. While you can mitigate as much as possible, you know that once you step onto the pitch, court, or track, you need to be able to adapt and respond to whatever your competitors throw at you.

In 1993, Jana Novotna faced Steffi Graf in the women's Wimbledon final. She lost the first set in a tiebreak, but took the second set 6–4. With Novotna 4–1 up in the final set, most people had written off Graf. However, Graf learned from what was happening, adapted her game play, and went on to win the final set, taking the title from a devastated Novotna.

Az's take

Match point

When I was younger, I played tennis at a reasonably high level. I was competing in one of the UK's largest tournaments outside Wimbledon and was seeded No. 3 for my age group. I reached the semi-finals of the competition, and came up against an unseeded player. On paper, there was no way that this kid should have beaten me. I was training four to five times a week to his once a week; I played at a national level and he wasn't even playing at a county level, but still he had beaten other good players to get to me in the semi-final.

I remember feeling good in my warmup, striking the ball well and analysing his play. I thought I could see where his weaknesses were and I was confident. In the first set, I went 4–0 down. I had no idea what was happening, so I decided I had to do something drastic and completely change my game to something I would never normally do.

I started slicing every shot, so I was striking at speed and low on the grass court, and he couldn't play those shots. I ended up winning the match 6–4, 6–0 because of my ability to adapt and change to a situation I hadn't foreseen. However, it could very easily have been a different story.

What allowed me to adapt and change my game was the fact that I trained so much more than my opponent and, despite not being the most talented player, I was more skilled because I had put in a lot of work to get there.

When it comes to being an adaptive organisation, you have to put in the work to get there. You need to do your own "training" and put all the things in place that we have talked about so far in the book. These are your foundations and they are what will allow you to pivot and course correct from a place of strength when you come up against circumstances you haven't seen coming and that are out of your control.

Fear versus determination

"You're only as good as your second serve" is a quote that's attributed to both Agassi and Sampras. Their point is that, in tennis, the second serve is normally where players hold back, but it's those who have the courage to push forwards who are more likely to succeed.

When you are in a situation where your back is against the wall, your mindset shifts, and you either have a mindset of fear or a mindset of determination. In sports, there are many stories about people and teams coming from behind to win under unlikely circumstances, but what allows them to dig deep is their determination to win. The example we shared of Steffi Graf beating Jana Novotna is one of many.

Rich's take

Mind over matter

I enjoy playing golf and, for many years, I was a six handicap and the best score I had ever got was four over par. One day

(continued)

(continued)

as I turned the first nine, I was two under par. By the time I reached the 15th hole, I was level. All I needed to do was finish the last three holes of the course at no more than one over par to achieve my best-ever score.

I thought, "Go defensive, just get par or one over … ". I got six over par on those final three holes. My whole mindset shifted when I was on track to get my best score ever and, where the mind goes, the score follows.

Having the right mindset is crucial when it comes to adapting as a business and staying the course, even if the route ahead might be uncharted for you. The challenge is to make sure that when the chequered flag goes up and the metaphorical finishing line is in sight that your mindset doesn't shift and undo all your good work up to that point.

The game is never over

We have talked about mindset in relation to sporting events when, of course, there is an end point. However, in business the game is never over. Even when it looks like an organisation may be down and out, there is often a way back if it makes bold decisions.

IBM is a classic example of this. In the early 1990s, the company was in a lot of trouble. It had lost its way, Microsoft was absolutely smashing it in the personal computer space and the predictions for its future were skeptical. This is when Lou Gerstner came in as CEO. He was a complete outsider, but he very quickly changed the dynamics of the business, got the company back on track, and put it on the path that it is still on today.

The same can be said for the Formula 1 team Mercedes AMG Petronas. Before 2014, the last championship it had won was back in the 1950s, until the arrival of Toto Wolff as director and team principal in 2013. Since then, Mercedes AMG Petronas has gone on to win seven straight Formula 1 championships. Thanks to Wolff's bold decision making and long-term vision, Mercedes' legacy has written its name into sporting history forever.

Especially as businesses grow, it's important that they find the right balance between innovation and process. In the book *Loonshots*,[3] Safi Bahcall talks about how young businesses are full of artists who are creative. They have loads of ideas and they believe anything is possible. However, when a business reaches a certain point, they bring in the soldiers, who are there to institutionalise procedures and put processes in place. To drive growth, Bahcall illustrates the need to manage the balance between artists and soldiers, or the soldiers can stifle innovation with processes and procedures.

This ties back into Rich's golf story and this concept of changing mindsets. In sports, this is when you go from an attacking mindset to a defensive mindset. You believe you've done what you need to win and you change your strategy. In business, when the artists get taken over by the soldiers, the business changes and, in some cases, it can plateau or even go backwards.

When this happens, what is often required is a new leader who can change the dynamic of the business, like Lou Gerstner did at IBM and Toto Wolff did with Mercedes AMG Petronas. Lego is another example referenced in *Loonshots* of a business that plateaued but, under innovative new leadership, has gone from strength to strength.

In a successful business like Lego, it can be tempting to start to submit to processes. The mindset can become one of, "Let's lay a

[3] Safi Bahcall, *Loonshots*, Macmillan USA International ed. (26 March 2019)

foundation to institutionalise what we've created, to keep this going for the next 100 years." This is a soldier's mindset, and it doesn't allow the artists to flourish and continue to innovate. What you need is a healthy balance between the two, where there is structure and process, but also the ability to innovate and push forwards.

Az's take

Attack is the best form of defence

I was coaching our ice hockey team, which was playing against a team that was significantly better. This team had ex-professional players and they were all over us in our zone. Our team was collapsing on the opponents and that meant all five of our players started to surround our net to stop things getting through. They automatically went into defence mode.

Because they were collapsing and just defending, our team allowed the other team to encroach on it even more. I told our team that one player had to hang on the halfway line and, even though at this point some players were unhappy with the change of tactics, I told them to trust me.

What happened as a result of having one of our players on the halfway line was that the other four players who were in our zone boxed up and created a defence that was more spaced out and that had structure, and it meant that our opponents needed one of their players to hang back and mark our player on the halfway line – meaning it also reduced the intensity of their attack. We ended up creating an attacking formation and this evened out the game.

This example ties back into the idea of making the right decisions, but also of making some bold decisions. There are times when, as a leader, you have to do something innovative or different, and you need your team to trust you and roll with your decision.

What about the environment?

We talked earlier about the effect that the weather can have on a Formula 1 race, and the story at the beginning of this chapter was all about how to use the weather to your advantage in business. Weather has an impact on businesses in more ways than you might initially think, and that is certainly the case with marketing.

British weather is notoriously changeable, so you can't rely on the seasons as a guarantee that you'll have hot or cold weather. A client of ours produces alcoholic beverages and, one summer, we created a marketing campaign that used data fed in from the Weather Channel. Our marketing messages would change based on that data. So, if the weather was hot, we would say, "Enjoy our product on ice." If the weather was wet or cold, we would say, "Enjoy our product in a hot chocolate."

We knew that we couldn't control the weather, so we adapted our strategy according to the context of what the environment was doing. There are some things that you can't affect; the sun will always rise and it will always set. What you have to do as a business is make sure that you're allowing for those elements that are completely out of your control but ever present.

It is also important to consider those factors when you are analysing your historical data. In the early 2000s, there was a fuel strike in the UK. The motorways around London and elsewhere in the country were gridlocked and no one was driving anywhere. Three years after this event, we were analysing data for a leading UK holiday resort and noticed that there was a significant blip in its village participation at this time. The reason was that no one could drive to the villages because of the fuel strike.

However, had we not had that knowledge to contextualise the data, we could have made all kinds of misleading assumptions about why the business suffered at that particular point. It was a similar story for a leading pizza restaurant chain in 2008 when the severe snow storms shut down most of the country and prevented people from going to its restaurants to eat. Its business took a hit and, looking at that a few years later, you needed the context of the snow to explain that drop in revenue.

The lesson here is that when you look at data historically, unless you have a way of also collecting and recording those external events, it can create havoc within a business. If you don't record events like these so that you have this external context to explain performance, then over time you lose visibility of them.

Highlights

There are a multitude of things outside of your control as an organisation: the pace of change, the economy, your industry, your competitors, consumer behaviour, even the weather. You might not be able to see everything coming, but you have to be able to respond no matter what does appear.

When you are an adaptive organisation, you have the confidence to pivot and change what you're doing, and you make decisions quickly. All too often, businesses make decisions from a place of fear or, worse still, become paralysed by the fear of making the wrong decision and therefore make no decision at all.

Everything we have discussed so far in this book aims to help you better understand your transformation into an adaptive organisation. To handle all of these elements that are outside of your control, you need to be confident in your abilities and to have built up your capabilities to allow you to pivot and change direction as required.

The mindset within your business, and particularly among your leaders, is crucial to enable you to take those bold decisions, continue to innovate, and in doing so drive progress. As we've seen through the various examples in this chapter, mind over matter can be a significant advantage when it's used from a place of determination, or a significant disadvantage when it's used from a place of fear.

In the final chapter of this book, we're going to bring together everything we've discussed so far and look at how, when you have transformed into an adaptive organisation, you can not only afford to go for a more daring shot, or to use a golfing term meaning three under par, the "albatross", but also that you're more likely to get it.

Chapter 8

Go for the Albatross

Identifying big opportunities and finding the confidence to grab them

"If you're always trying to be normal, you will never know how amazing you can be."

– Maya Angelou

W e're starting this chapter in 1935, on the final day of the Augusta National Invitational golf tournament, which is now known as the Masters. Craig Wood, tournament leader, had finished his round three under par and was relaxing in the clubhouse, with what felt like a very comfortable lead.

Gene Sarazan heard the spectators cheer Wood's birdie on the final hole as he was teeing up for his shot on the 14th. At that point, he was three shots behind Wood. Walter Hagan, his playing partner, turned to him and said, "Well, Gene, that looks as if it's all over." To which Sarazan replied, "Oh, I don't know, they might go in from anywhere."

His prediction came true just one hole later. It was on the 15th hole, a par five, that Sarazen took what was later dubbed "the shot that was heard round the world." He selected a No. 4 wood from his bag and carefully eyed the distance from the tee to the green. He knew he was going for the shot in two. His first shot put him opposite the green, with a small pond and a distance of 235 yards separating him from the hole.

Sarazen took one final look, breathed in, and hit the ball, which sailed across the pond, rolling neatly onto the green and down into the cup. A stunned silence was followed by cheers from the few spectators still watching. He had holed it in two.

In golf, an albatross is three under par. This score is only available on holes of par four, five, or six. The chance of hitting an albatross is at least one in a million. To put that in context, the chance of a hole in one is one in 2 500 if you're a pro and one in 12 000 if you're an amateur.

The boy who delivered the message of the albatross to the clubhouse that day in 1935 was greeted by considerable scepticism initially, with some of those present questioning whether he meant Sarazen had hit a two on the 16th hole, a par three.

Of course, the messenger had named the correct hole, and Sarazen had indeed hit an albatross. He went on to make par on the three remaining holes, tying with Wood and forcing a 36-hole playoff, which he won to take the 1935 Masters title. Sarazen used his considerable skill to follow the usual path to the green, but he did so in a way that pushed the limits and thereby enabled him to make up the ground he had lost to Wood.

Many would call this lucky, but as one of the greatest golf players ever, Gary Player, said, "The funny thing is, the more I practice, the luckier I get."

To get an albatross you need two things: length and skill. Most par fives have a shot at an albatross, but the reality is that only 10% of golfers can hit a par five in two shots. That means 90% of people never even have a shot at an albatross. To get into that 10% you have to build your capability and your skill. When you do that, the better the length on your shot, and the better your chances.

The same is true in business. Essentially you're stacking the deck in your favour if you put into practice everything we have talked about so far in this book. What you're doing is laying the foundations to allow you to go for the albatross.

If the principal has played her role, you have clear purpose and direction. If you've developed autonomy within your teams, set clear measures and created alignment with what you need to do, your crew is in place and ready to support your organisation on its journey. If you've considered the external environment, understand your role within it, and how it affects your organisation, then you have effectively set yourself up to be an adaptive business.

If you are an adaptive business, you can not only afford to go for the albatross, but you're more likely to get it. What's more, having done everything we've talked about in this book, you might as well go for the albatross because even if you don't hit it, you have the skills required to course correct, navigate your way out of the rough, and probably still get down for par.

The quote from Gary Player referenced earlier makes another important point, in that the more you practice, the luckier you get. The same holds true in business, in that the more you work on developing your capabilities and skills, the easier it will become for you to spot the opportunities for your albatross and the more confident you will be at having a realistic chance of hitting it.

There is one golf shot that's even rarer than an albatross and that's a condor, which is four under par. When you go for an albatross, you need skill and length, but you typically still follow the fairway. However, to go for a condor you have to cut the corner, and essentially hit the ball from the tee onto the green by the hole. If you can hit your shot that far, and you manage to land it in a very small spot, you have a shot at a condor. This shot is so rare that the PGA doesn't even have odds for it and there have only been a handful recorded in the world.

The difference between going for an albatross and going for a condor is that, if you have put in the practice, you have a realistic chance of hitting an albatross. If you miss it, you will probably still get a birdie (one under par) because you will have the skills to navigate out of the rough you land in. Even with lots of practice, hitting a condor is nearly impossible. As this shot is only available on par five and par six holes, there are also fewer opportunities for you to even attempt one.

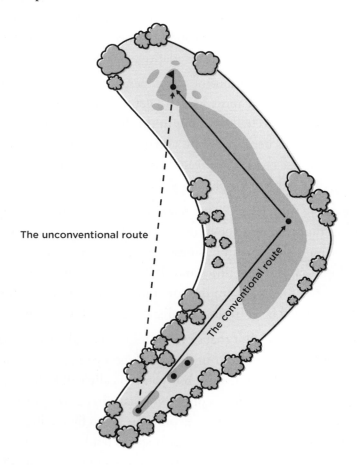

Figure 8.1

Knowing when to take the risk

Even if you are in a strong position, going for the albatross is still a decision that carries a certain degree of risk. A team principal may need to take a similar decision during a Formula 1 race if they are so far behind that the only way to close the gap is to opt for a risky strategy, like not coming into pit again to change the tyres. That 20 seconds can be the difference between making up the gap and falling farther behind.

The only way that a principal can make that decision is if they trust their car, their driver, and their crew. The team has invested in that technology and invested in that driver's training. It knows that it is operating well, and it is this knowledge that gives the principal the confidence to choose a risky strategy. Although this analogy only applies over the course of a single race, the principle is still the same in business.

You've earned the right to opt for the risky strategy by building up your confidence in the car, the driver, and the team. If you go for that strategy and it pays off, you have closed the gap, and now your job is to make sure you don't fall behind again.

This doesn't mean you should always choose the risky strategy simply because it gives you an opportunity to make up lost ground. There is a crucial difference between going for the albatross and cutting corners. While the act of going for the albatross might see you cut across part of the course, it is a calculated risk that is taken from a position of strength.

You have invested your time and effort in your training; you didn't cut corners when you were practicing, and you focused on continuously improving your skills and the length you could hit the ball. Therefore you know you have the skill and ability to potentially make the shot. As we have said earlier, even if you don't land where you want to, you also have the skills to course correct.

There is a fine line between bravery and naivety though. We recently saw a video of a pro golfer who hit a ball through a narrow gap between two trees and went on to get an albatross. Although both of us are keen golfers, we also know that we don't have the skill to make that shot. We would never manage to get our golf balls through that gap, and if either of us attempted that shot, it would be stupid.

However, that pro golfer could afford to be brave because he knew he had the experience and skills to give him a good chance of making the gap in the first place, and of being able to correct if it didn't go quite to plan. He had earned the right to go for the albatross.

Playing for the win, rather than the draw

When you go for the albatross, you're playing for the win. You're not aiming for a draw. This is all about recognising opportunities when they come along and seizing those opportunities when they appear.

In business, this might be in a type of David and Goliath scenario. Small organisations are often competing against much bigger businesses. While this might not quite have the drama of David stepping up to face the giant Goliath with just his slingshot and a few pebbles, the challenge can feel significant. However, a small organisation can be a disruptor and change its industry if it goes for the albatross at the right point in its journey. The small organisation can also use an albatross to gain an advantage over a much larger competitor. Think back to the brown rhino versus the elephant; small businesses can be the brown rhino in that scenario and surprise larger organisations that haven't seen them coming.

There is a similar battle between fast and slow. Large organisations can also become disruptors in their industry if they act quickly and decisively. The key is to make the right decisions and to make those decisions really count.

In 1996, in a football match between Manchester United and Wimbledon, a 21-year-old David Beckham put himself well and truly on the map. The decision he took towards the end of the match to go for goal from just within his own half led to not only one of the most memorable goals in Premier League history, but also put the young up-and-coming player firmly in the spotlight.

At that stage in his career, Beckham was one of a group of incredibly talented young players coming through the Manchester United ranks. He was quietly solid, but he didn't especially stand out from the likes of Neville, Scholes, Butt, Giggs, not to mention the huge personality of Cantona. That goal from just past the halfway line changed everything. It accelerated his career, his confidence levels went through the roof, and the rest, as they say, is history. In 2021, his net worth was estimated at $450 million. Of course, he has taken other decisions at other points that have continued to propel his career, both within and outside of football, but you could argue that his decision to go for that audacious goal in 1996 set him on that path.

Just as we discussed with the golfing examples, Beckham earned the right to go for that goal. He put in the hours of practice; he developed his skills, and that gave him the confidence to take the opportunity when he saw it.

We're sure you're familiar with the Chinese proverb: "A journey of 1 000 miles starts with a single step." The single step for Beckham wasn't that goal against Wimbledon; it was the training and practice he put in years before he got there that gave him that opportunity. He laid his foundations so that when the opportunity arose, he could take it. He also knew that the worst that would happen was that the ball would go out for a goal kick or be picked up by Wimbledon's keeper.

"In some brands there is a 'play it safe' mindset, and secondly a lack of innovative thinking. Some brands are so well established that at times they see opportunities that are new or untried to be a bonus or a chance to achieve extra, rather than necessary to maintain what they have.

Some people and brands are not looking to do more or be leaders, but to do the bare minimum, in some cases for perceived longer term stability and being too afraid to 'rock the boat'. These will be the brands that will not be here in 10 years."

Aaron Bradley, VP of Technology & Innovation, Wella Company

What's the worst outcome you'll get?

When you are making the decision to go for an albatross, one of the most important questions to ask yourself is, "What's the worst outcome if I miss?" In 2009 at the World Athletics Championships in Berlin, Usain Bolt said exactly that.

Having won gold and set a new world record in the 100m final, he was lining up in the 200m final as a firm favourite to take home the gold. In a post-race interview, he said that he had told his team he was going to go for the world record, even though he wasn't sure he'd get it as he felt tired after his 100m race, because the worst-case scenario was that he'd still get the gold.

Of course, his run on that night has gone down as one of the most incredible in history, with Bolt running 200m in 19.19 seconds, breaking his own record of 19.30 seconds that he set just a year earlier at the Olympic Games in Beijing. Even if Bolt had missed out on the world record, he would still have won the race by a considerable margin. When that is your worst-case scenario, it is certainly worth going for the albatross.

However, businesses need to understand what the worst outcome could be so that they can assess whether that worst outcome is something they can come back from. At the beginning of 2019, Gillette launched a new advertising campaign called "The Best Men Can Be", a play on its famous advertising slogan: "The Best a Man Can Get", and one that referenced the #metoo movement.

At the time of this campaign, Gillette's market share among younger consumers was coming under significant pressure from disruptors in the sector such as Harry's and Dollar Shave Club. Gillette took a bold decision to focus on the diversity, equality, and inclusion (DEI) angle in its advertising and it got it wrong. There was considerable backlash against the brand's attempts to reposition itself. In its first 48 hours on YouTube, the advert was watched two million times and received 23 000 likes and 214 000 dislikes.[1]

However, the strength of the brand allowed the company to course correct and make adjustments to its strategy. Even though Gillette took a hammering in 2019, two years later the business has launched its own direct-to-consumer operation. Gillette could afford to go for the albatross, and miss spectacularly, because it had laid the foundations for the business, it had brand equity, and although it temporarily lost market share, it knew it could regain it.

Gillette also chose to act early. DEI was gaining considerable traction at this time, and rightly so. Ethically, changing its advertising and branding was the right thing for Gillette to do, but because it was an early adopter, it wasn't executed quite as well as it could have been.

Contrast that to one of the disruptors in this space, Dollar Shave Club. As a Digitally Native Vertical Business (DNVB), it used a really strong, personally driven social campaign when it was building its brand and this pushed the company to the level that it is at now.

[1] Michael Baggs, "Gillette Faces Backlash and Boycott over '#MeToo advert'", *BBC* (15 January 2019), available at: https://www.bbc.co.uk/news/newsbeat-46874617

That was its albatross, and the company made it. If it had missed the mark, like Gillette did, the business would likely have ceased to exist because it didn't have the same solidity as Gillette.

Do you have to go early to land an albatross?

The short answer is "No, you don't." If you look at the Gillette example we just shared, you could argue that had the company waited a little longer, it might have had a better outcome from an updated campaign that was executed more smoothly.

There are also numerous business examples where being first doesn't equate to being successful. Myspace and Facebook illustrate this perfectly. Myspace was launched first, and at one point was the world's largest social networking site. Facebook was launched later and took a staggered approach to its launch, initially only making the platform available at Harvard, then universities, then later everyone else.

How many people do you know with an active Myspace account, compared to people with an active Facebook account?

Sometimes waiting longer can allow you to go for gold, especially if you watch the shots your competitors take and course correct based on their misses; think back to the pirate ship battle discussed in Chapter 4. By watching where their adversaries' cannonballs landed, pirates could adjust the angle and direction of their guns to improve the accuracy of their own shots.

In the business world, an example is how the iPod took over from the MP3 player. After the cassette-based Walkman and then portable CD players, MP3 players were a revelation. However, although they offered a much improved experience based on what was available before, they weren't always easy to use and they certainly had their limitations.

The Apple iPod was launched in 2001, several years after the first MP3 players came onto the market. One of the iPod's defining features was the wheel control you could use to scroll through your music. It was simple to use and it solved many of the issues consumers had with the early versions of MP3 players.[2] Apple waited, watched what its competitors were doing, saw where the competition missed its shots, and adjusted its trajectory accordingly. It took a little longer, but Apple went for the albatross and it got it. The company not only launched at the right time, but it also went for the big prize. While the decision itself is important, so too is the timing of that decision.

"The digital revolution we're seeing right now isn't about shiny new gizmos and tech toys. It's about progress: making things that improve and enhance all our lives. It takes maintaining the flexibility we learned in 2020 and changing our mindsets from caution to ambition. Making sure we're ready to keep up with the pace of change that customers and communities are driving. Understanding where they're heading and what's going to stick around."

Nicola Mendelsohn, CBE, VP GBG, Meta

When to go for the albatross

Whether you go early or later, the key is knowing when you can afford to go for the albatross. The following matrix highlights at what stage a business can go for an albatross with some degree of confidence. The horizontal axis relates to an organisation's maturity

---

[2]John Maeda, *The Laws of Simplicity*, MIT Press (August 2006)

(are you a spider or a starfish?), which is based around everything we've discussed to this point. The vertical axis relates to how you behave in business: Do you lead, follow, or hesitate?

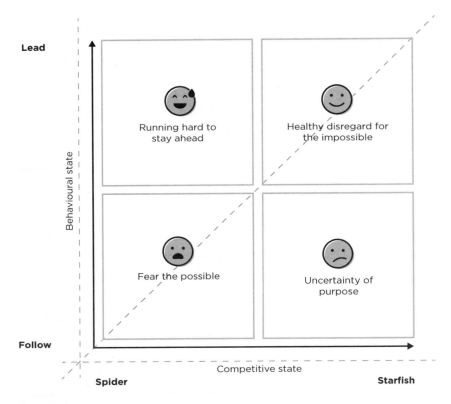

Figure 8.2

As you can see, you can be an agile business but not be overly confident in your ability to lead. As an agile follower you can still be in a very good place. However, if you want to make it into that top right-hand corner where you're adaptive and leading, you need a healthy disregard for the impossible.

Industry leaders don't ask for permission, they simply go for the albatross. She simply goes for the albatross. Not every organisation will be in a position to do that, but what this demonstrates is that you can still do well if you move into that space of being an agile follower. However, if you are a traditional, hierarchical organisation and you're following, you are likely to be more dependent on what everyone around you is doing.

Businesses like Tesla are what we would describe as adaptive leaders. They are early adopters and first movers; they go for the albatross and, more often than not, they get it right. If you look at the Tesla electric cars as an example, the company knew that there was always going to be some criticism and backlash to this new technology, but it focused on getting certain elements absolutely spot on, such as the innovation in the battery design, the design of the cars themselves, and the fact that they made a lot of what they were doing open source.

By getting those elements right, Tesla was able to mask the negative surround sound that accompanied this new technology, which, in turn, has elevated its performance moving forward. Tesla used its first mover advantage to shoot for the albatross, but it lined up its shot in such a way that it increased its chances of getting it.

Go for 10× not 10%

Part of going for the albatross is having the courage to make bold decisions rather than playing it safe. Google co-founder and former CEO Larry Page runs his business on the principle of 10×. He believes that a business should focus on making a tenfold improvement, rather than a 10% improvement. The point here is that if you are going for a 10% improvement, you are choosing the safe option and you are doing what everyone else is doing. While you won't fail spectacularly, you also won't wildly succeed. Essentially, when you take this course you are choosing not to go for the albatross.

As Steven Levy put it, writing for *Wired* after interviewing Page about his approach: "Thousand-percent improvement requires rethinking problems entirely, exploring the edges of what's technically possible, and having a lot more fun in the process."[3]

This is all about having a healthy disregard for the impossible. That means, as a business, you have to think about the best way to be able to solve a problem rather than thinking about the problem the same way everyone else is. When you have this healthy disregard for the impossible, you're in that top-right corner of the grid. You're shaping the future.

As one of Rich's energetic Peloton instructors says, "Shoot for the moon and, if you miss, you'll at least land in the stars." While this isn't strictly correct in terms of astronomy since the moon is 239,000 miles away and the closest star is four light years away, the sentiment is still relevant for both businesses trying to get ahead and businesses that are looking to catch up. Whilst optimisation is good, disruption trumps optimisation.

The other important point about the 10× principle at Google is that Larry Page has embedded it within the organisation. He wants all people at Google to embrace that principle, regardless of the level they're working at in the business.

In this case, the principle has been set and is clear within the business. Autonomy is embedded in Google's teams and it's functioning well; people have the freedom to think creatively to aim for that 10×. This means that the idea of going for the albatross isn't just part of the mindset of an organisation's leaders, but is part of the mindset of anyone working for that organisation. Everyone at Google is looking for 10× rather than 10% and that means people are seeking out their own opportunities to go for their own albatrosses.

---

[3] Steven Levy, "Google's Larry Page on Why Moon Shots Matter", *Wired* (17 January 2013), available at: https://www.wired.com/2013/01/ff-qa-larry-page/

Wins aren't always short term

It's important to remember that, unlike in a game of golf where you can see whether you have landed a shot within seconds, in business your wins won't always be short term. Sometimes you won't see the results immediately. In some cases, it is more like a war of attrition, the outcome of which is based on a set of decisions that you take over a period of months or years.

When you start looking at wins on a long-term timeline, you also have to consider when you should tap out versus when you should continue. Take the longest tennis match in history, which took place at Wimbledon in 2010 between John Isner and Nicolas Mahut. It took 11 hours and five minutes for Isner to win a match that spanned three days with a final set score of 70–68.

In his next match, Isner lost in straight sets in just 74 minutes to Thiemmo de Bakker, which at the time was the shortest men's match in Wimbledon history. The effort of winning his previous match significantly affected Isner's performance in his subsequent match. Of course, he still achieved a world record and being part of that match was a phenomenal achievement; however, a similar business scenario may have required a different decision.

As a business, you need to be able to work out when it is worth putting the effort into that war of attrition and when it's time to pull back. This links back to what is talked about in Chapter 3 in relation to the process you use for strategising and decision making within your organisation.

You can't cut corners when you're building foundations

One place where you need to put in the time and effort is in building your foundations. This is a point we have mentioned before, but it is absolutely crucial if you want to have the opportunity to go for the albatross with the confidence that you could land it, or at the very least know that attempting it won't be the death of your business.

When it comes to building your foundations, you can't cut corners. You have to put in the work, but that doesn't mean you have to do what everyone else is doing. You can think creatively and look outside the box for solutions. You simply have to make sure that the foundations and learning you have are based on the outcomes you want.

This might mean following the well-beaten path at times; however, you can take a detour as long as you make sure that your focus is always on the outcomes. When your learnings support your outcomes, you can achieve them.

The Wright brothers are a great example of how you can take a shortcut by thinking creatively, without being detrimental to the learnings you have as your foundations. In 1901, they developed a wind tunnel to test the design of their aircraft wings after becoming frustrated by the results of their experiments with gliders.

At this time, everyone working to develop a plane was launching models off of cliffs and hills. The Wright brothers invented a wind tunnel, which was the most efficient way of gathering all the data (the learning) they needed to make changes to their designs and significantly accelerate their progress. They conducted tests in their wind tunnel between September and December of 1901, and at the end of that short period had the most detailed data available in the world at the time about the design of aircraft wings.

They made the process as simple as possible without over simplifying it. This shortcut put them ahead of everyone else working in their field. However, a shortcut doesn't always mean you'll get ahead, and this is certainly true if you haven't got the right foundations in place.

Az's take

You're disqualified

When I was about 10 or 11, I was among a group of four or five who were strong cross-country runners. We trained together for the inter-house cross-country race at school, and our training took us along part of Peddars Way, which is the longest road built by the Romans. Peddars Way is surrounded by farmland and, because we were all local and knew the area really well, we would cut through the farmland to get back from our training sessions more quickly.

This shortcut of ours would take 15 to 20 minutes off our run times compared to everyone else. All of us were fairly athletic and good runners, so our teacher didn't think much of the fact that we were so much quicker than our other schoolmates. On the day of the race, we took the same route we'd been taking in training, cutting across the field. However, unbeknownst to us, one of our teachers was waiting. As we popped out of the field and rounded the bush by the gate feeling rather smug, we suddenly clocked the teacher watching us. Our stomachs dropped, our smiles disappeared and, of course, we were disqualified.

The irony is that our shortcut was unnecessary anyway because we were still some of the fastest runners in our class and, in all likelihood, would have won the race had we trained properly and taken the right route instead of trying to cut corners.

What this goes to show for businesses is that it's not about the shortcut itself, but about the foundations you put in

(continued)

(continued)

place. Instead of using that shortcut on our training route, we could have been like the Wright brothers and looked for ways to make our training more efficient. We could have used a treadmill or varied our training runs.

In business this is about finding different adaptive or agile ways to approach projects or challenges. Chapter 6 discusses how Aviva brought people from different business functions, such as finance and legal, into agile teams. This is an example of how an organisation can think differently and lay strong foundations that allows it to take shortcuts further down the line.

This is also about choosing to invest in the right things and laying strong foundations in the knowledge that good things will come when you do.

In golf there is a saying, "Focus on the par and the birdies will come." A birdie is one shot under par, an eagle is two under par, and an albatross, as we've previously said, is three under par. The point is that par is actually pretty good, so if you can get par on a course, you've done well. Go for the par and occasionally you might get a birdie as well. When you've got enough birdies, you'll get an eagle. When you've got enough eagles, you can go for the albatross.

It's an incremental process. What you can't do is be hitting over par and then go for the albatross because then you're cutting corners. If you do that, you're just going to end up in the bush and be facing an almighty challenge to even get back on course.

In the context of business, when you go for the albatross, the purpose is clear but it's very unlikely that you will get there on your own. You need your crew to support you and you need to evaluate the conditions when you are ready to take the shot. This is a journey, and it's important to lay the foundations, get the knowledge, and have the awareness to hit that shot with confidence.

Once the destination is set by the principal, and the crew is aligned behind that outcome, the next step is to find the most efficient way to get there.

Keep things simple

When it comes to creating a focused strategy, it's important that it focuses on customer needs. "Everything should be made as simple as possible, but not simpler," is a quote attributed to Albert Einstein and one that is very apt in this context.

Simplicity boils down to two steps: Identify the essential and eliminate everything else. In the context of going for the albatross, this is about identifying the best route to the green or acknowledging that this might be a time when you instead chip away and reach the hole over a series of more incremental shots.

Knowing when to take that bold decision and go for the albatross is, as we've already said, about understanding your abilities and having confidence in them. It is important to admit when you don't have the ability to go for the albatross because then you will start to look for another way that carries less risk for your organisation.

This concept of making things as simple as possible, but not simpler is also about making sure your priorities lie in the right place. There is an urban myth that in the 1960s NASA invested millions of dollars into developing a pen that could write in space, while the Russians just used a pencil.

Although that is a myth, it is a great example of avoiding innovation for innovation's sake. There is a real-world example of this too, in that Fischer spent $1 million developing a pen that could be used under freezing conditions. However, this is a very niche market, so you have to question decisions to innovate at times if the use of that innovation will be very limited.

Businesses also struggle with this concept when trying to reach the holy grail of personalisation. One of the challenges is that person-alisation has different definitions within the business that firstly need to be aligned. After that, there is an ongoing programme of work for "more personalisation." The two things that businesses often neglect, however, is what is the value to the customer? And when does the value saturate for the business? It's crucial to consider these questions because personalisation is only valuable if there is an improvement to both.

What does your customer need?

Innovation for innovation's sake is an issue we commonly see in tech projects. Technicians will often focus on building the core function-ality that they want in their product without thinking about it in the context of what's important to the customer.

This comes back to the concept of "Does it make the boat go faster?" that is talked about in Chapter 2. You will be able to make an infinite number of tweaks to your product or service, but you always have to measure the impact of those tweaks. Your measure is "Does it make the boat go faster?" and if the answer to that question is "No," then spending time and money on that change is not a wise investment.

Rich's take

The killer form

Many years ago I worked with a software developer who cre-ated a form that he described as a "killer form." At the time, this developer was building an application for the business, and I was constantly going back to him with ideas of all these different features and functionality we could introduce.

Every time I shared an idea with him, his response was the same: "That's a great idea. Just fill in this form and I'll take a look at it." The form was about two pages long and included questions about not only what the feature or functionality was, but also what its benefit was and how it would work.

Of course, I didn't fill that form in for every idea I had because it's easy to come up with 100 ideas a day, but it takes a lot more time to fill in two pages for every idea. That form always made me think about whether we really needed my idea, which was the software developer's plan. And if it was important enough for me to write two pages about it, then we would add it because we knew it would make the boat go faster.

Sometimes you have to strip back to go forwards

It can be easy to get carried away with adding functionality, as Rich just explained, and to introduce more and more layers of complexity to products or services. For businesses that have been around longer, this is likely to be particularly relevant.

However, sometimes you have to strip everything back to help you move forwards. You have to drop that deadweight because all of these things can slow you down. The key to doing this right is making sure that you strip back your technology or offering based on the need.

Az's take

Back to basics

I used to be head of user experience and performance at a social media company, where our lead developer was always enthusiastically developing new functionality. Often what he created was really cool and it worked really well, but the customer didn't always engage with it.

One of the things I proposed during my time there was stripping back the platform's functionality in what we called the "Do Less" project. It was focusing on improving the experience to users as simplicity was important because users would disengage and peel away if there was too much to think about.

I wanted to encourage our team to create a simple and smooth user experience, with the functionality appearing when it was needed, rather than us adding more and more functionality just because we could. Innovation was still important to us, but we pivoted as a team to focus on the outcome.

As Jeff Goldblum's character Ian Malcolm said in *Jurassic Park,* "You were so busy thinking about whether you could do it, you never stopped to ask if you should." It's a question worth posing more often in business, especially in the context of innovation.

Trust yourself, but apply the logic test

That question from *Jurassic Park* is an important part of the logic test, but there comes a point when you have the right foundations in place that you need to trust in your abilities and believe in your ideas to go for the albatross. US astronomer Carl Sagan once said, "They laughed at Columbus and the Wright brothers, but they also laughed at Bozo the clown."

People laughed at Columbus because the idea of finding a piece of land way across what they thought was a flat Earth didn't seem very logical. People also laughed at the Wright brothers because putting a piece of timber into the sky and flying it seemed ridiculous. But those people also laughed at Bozo the clown. Two out of those three things turned out to not be laughable at all.

There is a point with these daring albatross ideas where nobody knows if it will be a success. If you have laid the foundations we've talked about in this book then you have earned the right to trust what you believe in and to do it. Remember that until Columbus discovered America or the Wright brothers launched the first plane, there was no difference between them and Bozo the clown in the eyes of the public. The only difference was their own belief.

However, there has to be an element of logic to anything you are trying to achieve. If you compare the first plane, the Wright Flyer, with the rocket belt that was developed in the 1960s, you can immediately see how the first idea could logically evolve but the second could not.

When the Wright brothers launched their first plane, it only flew 200 yards; however, the laws of aerodynamics existed and were understood, so all they had to do to go from flying a plane 200 yards to flying it across the ocean was redesign the plane to change how those laws of aerodynamics applied.

When the rocket belt was first demonstrated, it flew for 21 seconds. However, the rocket belt needed one litre of fuel per second it was in the air. That meant if it was to fly for half an hour, it would need two tonnes of fuel. There was no way to make that better without changing the laws of physics.[4]

---

[4]Benedict Evans, *Not Even Wrong: Predicting Tech* (2020), available at: ben-evans.com

Some ideas can evolve to be successful and other ideas are waiting for bigger inventions in order for them to become practical. In business, you need to be able to make that distinction because your foundations will only take you so far.

This comes back to understanding your outputs versus your outcomes. If you launch something that can't be optimised thereafter, you have hit your limit. If that doesn't succeed on its first run it's never going to because you haven't given yourself enough runway to take off again.

There are many examples within the world of business where huge sums of money have been invested in ideas that, from the outside, are clearly destined to fail. When you look at those ideas, they typically all have one thing in common: Motion wasn't transformed into progress. However, everyone at that organisation got hyped up and excited so they didn't apply that logic test to what they were doing, and by the time they realised it wasn't going to work they had invested time and budget into a project that arguably should never have started in the first place.

Rich's take

Mortgage approved

In the early 1990s, I ran an R&D team for the largest bank in South Africa. One of the models my team worked on during that period was one to accelerate the mortgage application process with the bank.

In South Africa at that time, when you applied for a mortgage you would fill in the application with an estate agent, who would apply to four vendors, and you would take the mortgage from whichever of those banks came back with an offer first. The bank I worked for took 17 days to send a response after receiving an application. We were losing money hand over fist as a result.

The reason it was taking so long to respond to applications was that we would send an assessor to the property being purchased to assess the risk before we made a mortgage offer. As an engineering hydro-geologist, I was in my element building this model. We had access to statistics about rainfall, soil, and so on, and we created a digital map of every property in the country.

Our model, at the push of a button, could tell you the risk of a property having problems. If the risk was low, we could approve the mortgage application and send an assessor later to confirm. This model reduced our approvals process from 17 days to just one day.

During that time, we were competing with a large global consultancy that was also looking at ways to reduce our mortgage approval times. However, its system was never going to work. The consultancy started with a pilot at two of our bank's branches in Johannesburg, where they had a team of 30 people, each with a motorbike and handheld console, who would drive out to the property that needed to be assessed, evaluate it, and rushed the report back on a motorbike.

The bank had 600 branches across South Africa, so the thought of ever scaling that up to provide a viable, nationwide solution was insane. The mistake the consultancy made was in trying to evolve an inefficient process, using motorbikes and people, rather than thinking about how it could revolutionise the process to make it efficient in the first place.

(continued)

(continued)

This is where the logic test comes in for businesses. You have to ask whether a solution is scalable, and you also have to consider whether you are approaching the problem from the right angle.

Go back to first principles

First principle thinking is incredibly useful in this context. This is where you slow down, take something back to its simplest level, and build it from there. When you do this, you are much more likely to challenge an inefficient process and find a better way of doing things.

We see this happening a lot within startups and disruptors, particularly in traditional sectors like banking. Take the likes of Monzo and Starling as an example; from those apps, you can disable your credit cards at a touch of a button. You can pause them if you think you've lost them and you can cancel them if you know you've lost them. That functionality was built in from the start at those businesses.

However, the traditional banks, many of which offer that kind of functionality through their apps, took two years to get there. The reason being that their processes were so configured around the old way of doing things that they couldn't make quick decisions, even when they knew that those decisions were the right ones. The challenge for an organisation in this position is to take that step back and break the way you do things to enable you to make the change. If you're not able to do this, you're never going to lead, you will always be following others.

The following are just two examples of how a business that has been around for decades can benefit from taking a completely new approach to its customers. Both Zwilling Group and Volkswagen are well-established businesses that saw great improvements by viewing their challenges from a new angle and choosing to do things differently.

Cut above the rest

Zwilling Group is a 250-year-old business that manufactures and sells kitchen knives and other appliances. Over the years, it has had acquired other well-loved culinary brands, which resulted in a disjointed online experience for customers. In 2020/2021, the company underwent a significant digital transformation that connected the in-store and digital experiences, as well as bringing all of its brands together in one place.

In its stores, the company installed digital walls where customers could configure their products, so with a knife you could pick the colour of the handle, the size of the blade; you can even have it engraved and so on. Then you could select whether you want it delivered to the store or delivered to your home. This functionality is also available on the company's website.

This digital transformation has had a significant impact on the organisation's bottom line. In just three months, more than 50 000 new users joined the site, and sales in the US market alone climbed by more than 50%. There was a 6.9% increase in online orders across all its markets in the first three months the site was live.

(continued)

(continued)

The company has also focused on making its whole online journey informative and fun, so there is content about sharpening knives as well as cooking tutorials. This 250-year-old business probably has one of the most digitally engaging experiences available in this sector at the time of writing.[5] While it isn't always easy for older, legacy organisations to make significant changes and strip things back to the first principle, companies like Zwilling show that not only can it be done, but that it can be done well.

Are we nearly there yet?

As any parent who has had a long journey with children will tell you, it can be a challenge to keep them entertained at times. As a long-established automotive brand, Volkswagen (VW) is used to thinking about the customer experience from a driving perspective. VW recently developed a campaign called Road Tales that was designed to be more product oriented and to put the focus firmly on the people often travelling in their cars – families.

The company created a location-based interactive audiobook that is designed to transform long car journeys into magical adventures for children. It is available through an app, which transforms the scenery and objects children see outside the windows of the moving car into characters and locations in

---

[5] Isobar, "Digital Transformation: Zwilling", available at: isobar.com

a story, bringing the whole journey to life, and putting an end to the question every parent dreads, "Are we nearly there yet?"[6]

This was quite a significant shift for VW as a brand because it has always been focused on the cars themselves, rather than what is going on inside the cars when they are being driven. This campaign has won multiple awards and reached No. 1 in the app store within 24 hours of its launch.

In this campaign, VW stripped the experience back to the core audience it wants to reach, families, and thought about how it could improve their experience not just from the perspective of the driver, but also from the perspective of all the passengers in the car.

Highlights

If you want your business to be a leader in its industry, sometimes you have to go for the albatross. However, you have to make sure that if you take that shot, you have put all the foundations in place to give you the best possible chance of making it.

These foundations are everything we have explored in this book: the principal setting a clear direction, the crew that is aligned and operating autonomously to deliver its best work, and an appreciation for the season and what is happening that's outside of your control. When you have laid these foundations, you have earned the right to go for the albatross.

The other key is to think about the possible outcomes. What is the worst that will happen if you miss wildly? Think back to Chapter 3, which talks about classifying decisions and identifying the

---

[6]Isobar, "Road Tales: Volkswagen", available at: isobar.com

ones that could kill your business. As we've said in this chapter, there is a fine line between bravery and naivety, and you need to know which side of that line you are on before you go for your albatross.

An albatross can mean different things for different businesses too. The kinds of decisions an agile startup will be making are very different to those of a long-standing legacy business, but just because your business is larger, that doesn't mean it can't find its own albatrosses and use them to make up some of the ground it may have lost over the years, or use it as an opportunity to get ahead of the competition. This journey of transformation will be different for every business, and it is up to you to embed the principles we've explained in this book and take the right decisions at the right time to not only help your business catch up, but to also ensure it never falls behind again and consistently hits that podium position.

CONCLUSION

We started this book with an analogy of a rocking horse to demonstrate that motion doesn't always equate to progress. However, it is important to remember that there can be no progress without motion. If anything you've read in our book suggests that motion is not a necessity or is somehow a bad outcome, then that is an unintended consequence. The proverbial rocking horse comes into play when that motion is misdirected because this is when progress is not the outcome you achieve.

There is no right or wrong way to ensure that motion is directed as intended and that progress is always as expected. There are multiple ways to approach any project or challenge, not one track to follow. The key is to compare and contrast your options: are they efficient or inefficient; cost effective or expensive; enjoyable or exhausting; satisfying or a struggle?

Throughout the eight chapters in this book, we have explored a set of principles that you can adopt in your organisation to stack the odds in favour of progress being the logical outcome of your activities, regardless of the scale of the outcome you're focusing on. We have broken these down into what we believe are the three core themes of the business ecosystem: the principal (leader), the crew (team), and the season (enterprise environment).

In our Formula 1 team, the principal sets the priorities, the crew provides the momentum, and the season is the race schedule and environment in which each race takes place. As a business, you need leaders to be setting a clear direction and communicating the overarching purpose of an organisation or its initiative; your team needs to align with that purpose and have enough autonomy to perform at their optimum level; and finally, your organisation has to adapt to the wider environment and have the ability to pivot, otherwise your business can't stay ahead. When all three are aligned, you achieve progress. It is the combination that enables significant progress to be made because if even one of these themes is missing, it can lead to fatigue, chaos, or obsolescence for your organisation.

When you look at the best Formula 1 teams in the world, you can see how all three of these themes come together to enable exceptional performance and progress towards a desired outcome, whether that's to win the race on the day, or to gain additional points towards the broader championship race. In business it is no different. Your desired outcomes may differ from those of your competitors, but the commitment for progress towards defined outcomes will be the competitive advantage you need.

Shift gears to accelerate your progress

Among the key principles we have called out over the last eight chapters are the need to not only set a clear direction of travel for your organisation or initiative, but, also to find the right methods of measuring your progress. You need a strategy that is flexible enough to enable you to pivot and adapt as the world around you does the same.

Autonomy is a key concept in Part Two, where we explored the need for your organisational culture to support your team to work towards and deliver the progress you are striving for. This autonomy comes from alignment behind your organisation's purpose and a clear understanding of your direction of travel. In the final part of this book, we looked at how your business can become more adaptive, and the need to do so, to keep up with the ever-changing world we live in. You have to control what you can and be prepared to respond to that which you can't.

The main principles in Part Three focus on not only navigating challenges outside your organisation, but also in spotting the opportunities that these events present. Knowing when to go for the albatross can significantly accelerate your progress.

It is highly likely that you are already following a few, many, or even all of the principles we have outlined in this book. If you are able to implement even one more, your odds of a successful outcome should increase. While it is typically through the combination of these behaviours that success is compounded, we would caution against trying to boil the proverbial ocean. You don't need to try and win the battle on many fronts at the same time. Focus on improving one area, then move onto the next. In doing so, not only will your progress accelerate, but it will do so sustainably.

The key is to view each of these principles as a behaviour, and behaviour change can have a positive effect on both a small and a large scale. Although we have shared examples that span organisations, know that these principles are just as effective and useful for individuals as they are for C-suite teams. Our hope is that all who read this, regardless of their current position or the size of the organisation they work for, will find value in what we have shared and see opportunities to alter their behaviour to help drive meaningful progress.

Whilst writing this book, we would always joke about who was early or late to our sessions because we both believe that there is no such thing as being on time; you're either early or you're late.

It's the same approach we take with our clients. Often businesses will score themselves in a neutral way. For example, when asked to score something out of five, many people will pick three because it avoids being positive or negative. However, this can hold businesses back when assessing their own current state. We have talked about turning headwinds into tailwinds in Chapter 6. This is about assessing whether something is helping you move forward or holding you back as it is an important distinction.

Having the mindset to look at each of your capabilities and candidly say that "this is holding me back or driving me forward", is the key to knowing what changes are needed to transform motion into progress.

Throughout this book, we have created a set of exercises that are designed to spark ideas that are appropriate for your situation. We have not sought to create exercises that will solve specific problems because every situation and business is unique. The principles we have outlined can be tailored to suit any situation, and our hope is that as you work through these exercises, you are able to see how you can apply them to your organisation and move closer to becoming an adaptive organisation.

Our final exercise is to pull together all this information to help you better understand what is helping you or stopping you from making continuous progress. The difference in our approach to traditional maturity assessments is that we've tried to factor in the complexity that sits behind being an adaptive business. We have pulled together the information shared in this book from the principal, the crew, and the season to look at all the aspects in your business that we believe will help you transform motion into progress, whilst trying to recognise the value and complexity of the relationships among all of these capabilities.

Progress accelerator

We have an exercise on our website www.motionintoprogress.com to help guide you to get a view of your current state that aligns with your purpose and enables all of your teams to deliver the best possible customer experience.

We also hope that you have enjoyed reading this book as much as we have enjoyed writing it. If you take only one thing from what's included in these chapters and find it useful in your business, we have met our goal. If you take more, that is a bonus.

"Whilst motion without progress is common, progress without motion isn't possible. Transforming motion into progress is where you'll see competitive advantage."

Rich and Az

EPILOGUE

What our adaptive leaders have to say

Many of the leaders whom we were in contact with mentioned a set of common themes and challenges that businesses need to address to drive meaningful progress. The combined content across their vision and experience was so strong that we wanted to pull this summary together to give you a glimpse inside the minds of this incredible group of people.

The key themes that we chose to bucket their feedback into are:

- Put the customer first.
- Have an aligned purpose with strong values.
- Balance the C-suite perspective.
- Pivot from measuring what you can, to measuring what you should.

Put the customer first

The President of Consumer Products at a global media and entertainment organisation said, "A successful brand today needs to do what all successful brands have always done: focus on the consumer." She then went on to say:

"The consumer purchasing journey and what matters to them has changed over the last few years. A brand must stand for something and be consistent with its messaging, partnerships and activations."

The simplicity of keeping the consumer at the centre of brands is the foundation of why organisations need to become adaptive. The flexibility that is provided by enabling your business to better react and service today's increased consumer expectations will limit the chance of your organisation ever falling behind your competitors, and as this leader went on to say, "If a brand does this consistently, it will be profitable."

This is further supported by Aaron Bradley (VP of Technology & Innovation, Wella Company), who believes that "the biggest influencers for brands are their customers. Customers want brands to show that they understand their needs and know them as an individual." Aaron goes on to say that this includes not just requirements from brands' products and services, but also meeting the social and ethical requirements of consumers.

This theme of customer centricity is supported by Benjamin Braun (CMO, Samsung), who believes that the acceleration in digitisation at the start of 2020 was a catalyst for the need for better short-term customer personalisation and a real opportunity for brands to respond:

"As marketers, we now have the opportunity to grab the bull by its horns and make a greater impact with our work, driving sales as we boost customer experience."

Benjamin goes on to say that this comes from a close alignment of the business and the removal of organisational silos.

This breakdown of silos is key in making sure that there is alignment within the business that keeps everyone focussed on helping customers who are themselves adapting to the pace of change. Nicola Mendelsohn, CBE, who previously oversaw Facebook's operations for the entire EMEA region and recently became the global advertising chief for Meta's Global Business Group, believes that there's an evolution that's come from this opportunity to enrich the lives of customers:

The pandemic has shown us just how fast the pace of change can be. The things we're doing not just differently, but better, will stick around – and it's here that I think technology can be a powerful force for good. Because the digital revolution we're seeing right now isn't about shiny new gizmos and tech toys. It's about progress: making things that improve and enhance all our lives. It takes maintaining the flexibility we learned in 2020 and changing our mindsets from caution to ambition. Making sure we're ready to keep up with the pace of change that customers and communities are driving. Understanding where they're heading and what's going to stick around.

Have an aligned purpose with strong values

"Proper leadership is essential to keep people motivated towards a desirable outcome. Just read Working Backwards *to fully appreciate how Amazon has become the dominant player globally and is really only just getting going. There are loads of examples of culture that informs success, but it all starts with the leaders and the way they develop the people in a business to own it from the inside out. When this is done with authenticity and trust in the people, it becomes an unbreakable foundation for growth."*

– Craig Smith, Chief Brand Officer & Co-Founder,
Decidable Global Ltd, and Former Digital Commerce Director,
Ted Baker

There was a strong sense from the leaders here that they felt accountable for defining and aligning the business purpose and values with the rest of the organisation. Craig went on to say that whilst it can be a challenge getting all stakeholders and decision makers aligned on the direction of the organisation and the customer experience it needs to deliver, when done well, it will assist with driving the commercial numbers and customer satisfaction in the right direction.

Samsung's Benjamin Braun believes that to be successful and to genuinely push boundaries, you need this type of culture that is pulling in the same direction and is centred around innovation:

"That's what I enjoy the most but it can take different forms. At Samsung, we have a strong Korean culture – it is fast-paced, and success driven. The whole company empowers and enables staff to do their best work and is constantly looking ahead to the future. It is very inspiring."

Benjamin has explained that to achieve this, businesses need to break down the silos and encourage a more holistic approach to consumer engagement and business growth. Failing to do this may cause your organisation to fall behind its competitors.

Balance the C-suite perspective

One of the consistent themes through all our interactions with these leaders is the need for ensuring that tomorrow's C-suite has a balanced perspective, – one that embraces the pace of change and ensures that innovation and flexibility is baked into the strategic landscape for the business. This ensures that businesses don't just look at short-term profit, but balance that with longevity and a stronger focus on customer needs.

"We've seen a collapse of the traditional purchase funnel – the customer journey still exists, but it's no longer solely focused on that lower funnel purchase. People can be made aware of a product and purchase in just a matter of seconds. And this presents a real opportunity for brands to be meaningfully present in the spaces their customers are now occupying, which is increasingly digital."

– Nicola Mendelsohn, CBE, VP GBG, Meta

Short-term versus long-term planning

"A strong long-term strategy needs to be transparent and communicated well, making it clear what to expect and what short-term results look like, good or bad."

– Aaron Bradley, VP of Technology & Innovation,
Wella Company

So, how do brands balance the focus on short-term results with the need for long-term investment into the future? Paloma Azulay (Global Chief Brand Officer, Restaurant Brands International) says by *"working on both on the same time. Investing in the short term gives you quick wins, credits, and the breadth to take bigger actions in the long term (or buys you time). Still, there are many ideas that create short term business sales but also have a long-term impact. This sweet spot is very powerful."*

Brand versus data

"Data and content velocity are the most valuable weapons in a brand's arsenal, outside of their product and their people. More data provides them with a more complete view of their audience, which in turn allows for more personalised messages, but it's just as crucial to get those messages out to the right people at the right time to build and maintain strong customer relationships."

– Paul Robson, President of Adobe International, Adobe

Paul is passionate about how data can be the enabler for personalised interactions, providing an opportunity for businesses to meet at the intersection of brand and data to better meet customer needs, and be a force for good in doing that. This view was shared by Aaron from Wella Company, who believes that *"For a brand to be successful in the future and beyond, more areas throughout the organisation need to have the capability of interpreting the data and taking action. The speed at which customers are evolving means that brands need to be agile in changing their approach quickly."*

This is where brands have the opportunity to truly innovate and evolve their existing business:

"By capitalising on new technologies such as AR and VR, which are moving from experimental to mainstream, brands can offer customers a deeper sense of presence and connection."

– Nicola Mendelsohn, CBE, VP GBG, Meta

Pivot from measuring what you can, to measuring what you should

"There has never been more data available to brands and marketing teams about their customers. We're living in the age of data and measurement. But with so much data available, it's also difficult to cut through the noise to get to the insight. That's why you need a team with the right skills and right technology to start looking at where your gaps are and where your future investment should be placed."

– Paul Robson, President of Adobe International, Adobe

When we asked the VP of Marketing at a large American retailer "Why do you think brands are stuck measuring what they can rather than what they should?" she responded:

"It's much easier to measure what has happened in the past and big data systems have developed impressive precision to effectively translate that data into future models, spitting out forecasts that are well-validated and that can yield consistently 'green' scorecards. This feels very reassuring both when creating plans and also when the results come back, validating the strength of the model and accuracy of the

forecast. Most large companies and certainly Wall Street reward this accuracy and consistency. It's also easy to see if a model is 'good' or 'bad' in the more black and white sense that data science culture often rewards."

Revisiting the VP from our large American retailer, she also went on to say:

"It is much harder to model and forecast against new scenarios and contexts that we haven't seen before – and much of what it will take to win big in the future will require conquering these unknowns and navigating constantly evolving consumer and market contexts. Models to do this type of work and planning will not be black and white and will not be perfectly validated. There will be ranges and assumptions to be pressure tested and optimized. These 'grey' scenarios can make both data scientists and senior executives uncomfortable as the certainty of outcomes won't be there when some decisions need to be made. Winning in this scenario requires a blend of creativity, strategic thinking, and often times, a 'gut' in terms of where culture and people are headed. And most of all, it demands real bravery amongst leaders to take risks, knowing when you know 'enough' to go and when further learning is needed to balance risk/reward."

The role of measurement as a catalyst for change is often not maximised by businesses, and they end up with ambitious transformation visions that deliver undesirable outcomes because it's not possible to measure what really matters and keep all of these initiatives clearly on track. To be truly data driven in your decision making is an advantage that few businesses really use, and those that do reap obvious rewards.

"It's extremely common for brands to say they want to be data driven but the reality is that some continue to base their plans on what they do know and not what they could know. They use data to try to verify after the fact, not before making the decision."

– Aaron Bradley, VP of Technology & Innovation,
Wella Company

ABOUT THE AUTHORS

Azlan Raj is the Chief Marketing Officer for Merkle and dentsu's EMEA Customer Experience Management service line. His role spans all dentsu capabilities across commerce, data and technology platforms, analytics, media, customer experience, content, and B2B. He is responsible for continually evolving Merkle and dentsu's leading digital and data capabilities across the region to drive customer experience transformation for clients, helping them find the balance in blending brand and data through their customer experience. Previously the EMEA leader for Merkle's customer experience capability, he built the company's regional capability to over 1 200 people in just three years to help global brands transform their organisations to deliver more personal and data-fuelled customer experiences.

With over 20 years of experience in the digital industry, prior to joining Merkle, Azlan worked for leading brands, agencies and consultancies, including Barclaycard, Publicis Sapient, and Accenture. Through his career, Azlan has been part of award-winning teams and led a diverse set of capabilities from marketing strategy through to analytics, website design and development, and marketing activation. He is a recognised thought leader writing for mainstream publications and presenting at leading industry events including Forbes, Campaign, The Drum, PerformanceIN, Adobe Summit and Econsultancy, and is a member of the renowned Forbes Communications Council, Performance Marketing World Advisory Board and Data & Marketing Association (DMA) customer engagement committee. Azlan was also recognised in PerformanceIN's top 50 list for marketers.

Azlan is also passionate about the industry's efforts in the diversity, equity, and inclusion (DEI) space. He is actively involved in supporting Merkle's DEI pillars, and is especially committed to ensuring that inclusivity and social responsibility are embedded into today's communications.

Rich's take on Az

"Dreams are born in our heads, but they are forged in the fire of experience."

– Carol Tice

During the process of writing Shift, *Az and I have had to channel dreams born in two different heads, and forged across diverse experiences, into a 200+ page stream of mutual consciousness. This could test the strongest of relationships, but working alongside Az on this project has been one of balanced duality. Give and take. Share and build. Learn and grow.*
Az is from that rare group of people who excel at everything they do, accumulating learnings and experiences along the way, making him one of the most engaging storytellers I have had the pleasure of working with. He has an insatiable curiosity, fuelling a unique ability to balance art and science, and on top of all of this, still be a family man, putting the people in his life first.
We have combined our respective strengths on this project, and given Az the freedom to use his superpower – simplifying the complex, which in trying to synthesise ideas and content across such a multifaceted topic has been essential.
One of my favourite quotes has always been "it's never crowded on the extra mile" and I have found through this process that

> *Az lives right out there! Never was a hurdle too high, or a time*
> *Az wasn't totally focused on our goal.*
> *"Together" would be my simple summary of what the journey*
> *has been like. We have learned and grown through what has*
> *been a fun and fulfilling process, and I hope this is only the first*
> *edition!*

Richard Lees is Chief Strategy Officer for Merkle and dentsu's EMEA Customer Experience Management service line. His remit sits at the intersection of customer experience strategy, measuring what matters, omnichannel architecture and organisation transformation, to enable businesses to capitalise on the total customer experience. He plays a key thought leadership role that underpins the strategic and competitive positioning of the Merkle business across EMEA, and works collaboratively across both Merkle and dentsu to deliver this. Prior to this role, Richard was the CEO and co-founder of DBG, a marketing and technology consultancy that was acquired by Merkle in 2016.

Richard has spent more than 30 years applying data to solve a multitude of business challenges. In this time, he has been a founding partner of, grown, and sold two successful businesses, both of which focused on using data, technology and insights to optimise cross-channel customer communications. Working both on the client side and in his own businesses, Richard has had profound hands-on experience across myriad technology, data, analytics, decisioning, experience, strategy, and communications disciplines. He has been a regular speaker at numerous global industry events, a regular contributor to mainstream publications and was recognised in DataIQ's top 100 list for the most influential data and analytics practitioners.

Richard plays an active role in the execution of Merkle's DEI initiatives, leading the Lived Experience pillar, which is tasked with improving the daily experiences of our ethnic minority colleagues' lives. He is passionate about the power of diverse collaboration and the compound value of the shared know-how and experience of all our people.

Az's take on Rich

Professional baseball player Charles "Chili" Davis said that, "Growing old is mandatory; growing up is optional," and it's almost as if he was talking about Rich when he said it. Whilst Davis was talking about his passion for baseball, this quote acutely depicts Rich's years of experience, which is underpinned by a young heart.

Growing up in South Africa and moving to the UK, Rich had a diverse lifestyle which started as a curious young boy who would burn leaves through a magnifying glass at school, to learning discipline and structure through his mandatory service in the army, through to having his supportive family around him today. All of which contribute to the way that Rich thinks, acts, and draws on his experiences.

Rich has some unique talents, including an amazing ability to draw (and write) upside down whilst simultaneously explaining something, but I've had visibility of his superpower in full flight through our time working on Shift*: his brain. It works like lightning in a bottle; one spark can set off a series of thoughts that are processed at the speed of light. It's incredible to watch.*

If I were to reference our pyramid approach in this book and try to describe Rich in three words, they would be (super) smart, humble, and empathetic. Individually they are all great traits, but pulling them together, I can only describe as the intersection of genius; and Rich, in my view, is one of the best thought leaders in our industry with an unparalleled passion for helping businesses to turn motion into progress.

At a time when everyone has had their fair share of ups and downs, writing Shift *has been one of my favourite memories, and I've genuinely enjoyed and feel incredibly honoured to have worked with Rich on this book.*

INDEX